Dear Helen,

LOUISE GOODFIELD

Plant Your Poetry

365 Poems and Prompts to Grow Your Writing Habit

May your words blossom beautifully out of this book you deserve this.

All my love,

Louise

xx

COTTON FIELD PUBLISHING

You deserve this.

As you start to walk on the way,
the way appears.

Rumi

Contents

Introduction

It requires faith and patience to nourish and nurture plants. It's a gentle practice that requires daily attention. If I stepped outside never having tried gardening before and expected to know how to grow plants simply because I had hands, I'd waste a lot of soil, blame the plant, then myself, and give up entirely before the week was up. Being a gardener is much like being a poet, it's a great undertaking, responsibility, and joy, but it is first and foremost a discovery.

If someone had told me when I reached thirty-three that I'd work as a poet and spend my days writing I wouldn't have believed them. Unhealthy relationships, and trying to survive as an artist in London had me at breaking point. I spent too long trying to convince everyone (and myself) that struggling in London was a by-product of living in a place that 'had the most opportunities'.

I gave the impression that I was on top of everything but I wasn't. I experienced regular and disruptive health issues, and confidence in my decision-making and creative talents was at an all-time low. I was giving away my time for free and putting energy into projects that were serving others. I had no reserves for myself or for my writing. I thought if I could figure out the magic formula on how best to cope with the pressure - everything would be fine. Soon I was convinced that I was an unfixable problem, a weed in need of pulling out by the root.

Self-hatred was crushing my spirit and pushing me deeper into a rut. I held on so tightly to maintain control, but that made it worse. Finally, the universe took matters into her own hands. She wrenched everything I'd been clinging to out of my life and I was left looking at the wreckage wondering how on earth I'd ended up with nothing. My ego was bruised, I thought I was old enough to know better by now.

The one good thing about rock bottom is that the only way is up. The emptiness was terrifying, but it was also *thrilling.* For the first time, the pain of staying where I was felt greater than the fear of change and I knew that my life depended on whether I was willing to let go and listen to what was calling me.

When gardening, if a plant struggles to bloom, we don't blame the plant and demand that it produce a flower, we study its environment. We ask, what does this plant need to be healthy? So I left a ten-year career and moved to a small town I'd never heard of in a foreign country where I could barely speak the language.

Although the transition wasn't easy, the new environment re-awakened my childlike wonder. I fell in love with this new land, its people, and its culture. The streets were rich in colour, history, music, and dancing. Poems floated into my brain like half-remembered dreams and I scribbled them down as quickly as I could. The low cost of living meant I could afford 'a room of one's own' (my first ever solo apartment), and the slower pace of life meant I had time to face everything I'd been avoiding by keeping busy.

Although I agree that fortune favours the brave, quitting your job and moving abroad to begin your daily writing habit isn't compulsory. It's more about embodying a receptive state of being. *Be astonished and tell about it* as Mary Oliver would say.

In 2022 I joined a free Winter Writing Sanctuary run by the gorgeously generous and talented author Beth Kempton (Kokoro, Wabi Sabi, The Way of the Fearless Writer). This was my first experience being part of a large writing community where I could share my words. Comforted and supported by other people in the same boat, I started to unpick the emotional blocks and barriers that were hindering a healthy (and fearless) writing life. One of those barriers was *I'm not someone who can do that sort of thing.*

I joined a prompt challenge in 2023 called #tinyspringpoem run by Beth (thank you, Beth). Every day a prompt was shared and we wrote on that for ten minutes a day. The challenge finished within a month, but I'd found a groove and didn't feel ready to stop. Others wanted to keep going too, so I created more prompts and carried the torch for those who wanted to continue.

I never intended to write 365 poems in one year, doesn't that seem like a lot? But focusing on one simple goal, to write one poem per day, means I'm now *someone who can do that sort of thing.* It's been a journey, but one that has changed my life.

Audrey Hepburn once said *to plant a garden is to believe in tomorrow.* Whatever we plant, reaps fruit to feed not only ourselves but other hungry souls in need of sustenance. There are no fruits more delicious than those grown through creativity. So I gathered all I learned and put it into this book so you can see that it's possible for you too.

So if you're drowning in a non-existent writing practice thinking something is wrong with you, or the desire to write is eating you up from the inside because you can't start or stick to writing, this book will walk you towards a blossoming writing life.

Shall we begin?

How to Begin

What are the chances you're reading this sentence feeling rather inferior compared to the task ahead of you?

Me too.

It's ridiculous that I've written and published this book yet in the chapter titled 'How To Begin', I'm not sure how to tell you how to begin. But here I am, writing words, look at that, I've begun. Scribble a word or two on this page or in a notebook. Use the words, *I've begun*. If you don't have anything to write with or you're reading on a device, say it out loud. Now you've begun too.

The writing of poems isn't the hardest element of growing a writing habit, it's the emotional attachments and fears we must face to get to a place where we can begin. Take a moment to sit with any emotions or physical impulses that are bubbling to the surface. There is nothing wrong with the myriad of emotions that will inevitably show up, they all have their place. You've got this.

I hear a little voice creeping in. *Yeah right, how do you know?*

I'm the most inconsistent person in the world. I receive huge waves of inspiration that I need to recover from for twice as long as those periods last. I have around 200 poem starts in my Google Drive and about ten ideas for fiction books that may never see the light of day. Even as I sit down to write this paragraph, I've poured a glass of wine and checked my texts, grabbed a blanket, cuddled the dog and fed her dinner, stopped in my tracks to listen to the lyrics of the song 'Dreams on Fire' by Katie Melua and... sorry where was I? Oh yes. Queen of Distraction.

When carving time to put pen to paper, or choosing my writing over almost anything else, my boundaries are about as disappointing as a weak cup of tea. I'm the *last* person you'd expect to have written 365 poems in a year. But here I am. The journey I'm about to guide you through changed my life, but most importantly, it changed my *mind.* It changed my mind about what was possible. I know this may be difficult to believe when you're convinced that *you* are the world's worst when it comes to commitment. But you're here now, aren't you?

Here we both are. The whisper that brought us here is giving us the chance to change our story. The belief we hold about ourselves (that we haven't got what it takes to be a writer) is ready to be challenged and the only way to do that is to write that belief out of our system.

How are we going to do that?

Begin with DAY 1: PROMPT on whatever day this book lands in your hands. The word featured next to the number of the day is your poetry prompt. Set a timer for 10 minutes and write. Write first and worry about where the poems will end up later, you'll have plenty of time to sift back over them and edit or re-read them at a later date, each poem you write will open up a door to another.

If you're nervous about what to write when you get to the first prompt and struggle with a blank page, write through the uncertainty one word at a time. Write the prompt word repeatedly and any words associated with it that come out until you find some momentum.

Read the poem I've written on the prompt and if you need some support, use one of my lines to start you off. I wrote these poems using the same method to show you it's possible and help inspire you when you're feeling stuck. If you use a line from one of my poems and share or publish it, remember to write *'After [PROMPT TITLE], by Louise Goodfield'* under your title to credit it properly.

If you find yourself looking at my poems thinking *I'll never write like that*, be gentle with yourself and know that these poems have been edited to give you a good reading experience. I wanted this to be enjoyed as a full poetry collection as well as a writing companion. The unedited poems are scattered around the internet in various places and are full of typos and extra lines. So it's impossible to compare your poems to mine, and I'm glad you'll never write like me, the world doesn't need another poet like me, it needs you and your unique offering.

Look at the prompt word and poem in the morning and carry that word with you throughout the day. One of my favourite things about this process was that I began to see the world through the lens of the daily prompt and it anchored my writing, offering me many poem openings to choose from.

Choose a journal or a folder on your computer to keep all of the poems in one place, a lot can happen in a year and you may forget which prompts you've written on. This will help you when we get to the reflection prompts and journal questions towards the end of the book. I'd recommend using Google Drive. If you join the Plant Your Poetry Facebook group, which you can access via a link at the end of this book, your poems will be easily accessible using the #plantyourpoetry hashtag.

There are many ways to use this book. If working chronologically isn't working for you, run your finger down the contents page and stop when you feel like it, or open the book at a random page, take it as a sign, and write. Maybe you'll write some prose or a love letter. If it doesn't arrive as a poem, perhaps it wasn't meant to, maybe it's destined to be part of a blog or Substack essay, and that's okay.

Keep a discovery journal. Note down when you find writing difficult, or when you feel inspired. Keep track of the day, the prompt and what is going on in your life. Writing every day will make you a good resource on what helps or hinders your writing. Your future self will thank you when you feel like you've forgotten everything you learned, and perhaps someone else can benefit from the wisdom you'll gain.

We're almost ready to get going, but first I want to touch on a sneaky part of the writing process that preys on unsuspecting writers. It can be the most difficult part of the writing journey to navigate.

How to Keep Going

Even though there isn't a fail-safe way to write every day for the rest of your life, this book tackles two of the biggest fears we hold as writers: that we will never begin and that it's impossible to finish.

But what about the expansive gap in between? How do we keep showing up when we've planted our seeds but can't see anything sprouting through the soil? What if we fail? What if we give up? Our minds work overtime trying to fix the problems we believe could happen, and we begin negotiating with our inner critic who has decided they're going to protect us from harm, the one who normally tells us that the best way to avoid failure is to stop altogether or avoid starting.

Our inner critic will use several clever tactics to protect us from failing, the first is perfectionism. The more we try to attain perfection, the more others feel the need to keep up, it's a vicious cycle. Momentum starts to drop, the initial dopamine hit of starting something new fades away and suddenly we feel that we have to exceed expectations. This is the most dangerous part of the journey because it is the most easily excused by saying *hey, at least we tried*, but find yourself on the other side of this sticking point and you're running home free towards a fully-fledged writing habit.

Perfectionism isn't about making a poem perfect, it's about making sure it isn't *anything* if it's less than perfect. Writing isn't the same as maths, there is no set answer, and it's subjective and preferential. So if we allow our inner critic to reign as supreme judge over our lives to protect us from failing, what will it say? You should try something else.

Then the inner critic deploys their next strategy, procrastination. Suddenly we are doing everything but the one thing that makes us feel truly alive and free, the thing we ache for. The worst part? We think this means something is fundamentally wrong with us and we begin to tell ourselves, *I'm not someone who can do that sort of thing. I'm not a writer.*

Do you think you deserve that? No, you deserve more.

So thank your inner critic for caring about your health but politely decline its suggestions. Many, if not all writers at some point along their journey struggle with this conundrum. There is nothing wrong with you.

I didn't write 365 poems because I write perfectly, nor did I have the perfect life conditions that writers imagine everyone else has so that I could write this book. Perfectionism did not help me grow my writing habit, but there are a few things that did.

Making a small number of consistent tries helped me to make progress. Whenever I fell behind, I got back on track by re-focusing my attention on the goal: to write one poem for 10 minutes that day. Nothing more, nothing less. This was manageable. When I say 'back on track', I mean writing again. Letting go of the need to keep up with writing a poem every day, or with a certain quality of poem I wrote previously helped.

There were days when a prompt inspired me to look at an old draft poem in a new way and days when I could only write one line. I formatted it in an interesting way and these ended up being my favourite poems. I acknowledged my disappointment and replaced self-hatred with gratitude that I'd made an effort, and that was enough to keep me writing the next day.

Providing poetry prompts and sharing inspiration daily on social media held me accountable to the writing community. Connecting with others on the same journey helped me keep going when motivation was low or life got busy. Receiving personal messages and comments on my poems reassured me that I wasn't alone and that I was making a difference. This showed me that my words were not only valid but necessary and contributed to helping me shift from self-doubt into a more confident and active writer. So if you have a spare moment in the day to show another poet some love for their work, it will help to keep them going too.

If sharing your poems with thousands of people is nerve-wracking or you struggle with comparison, I'd recommend choosing one person you trust and inviting them to be your writing buddy. Start writing on the same prompt if you can and send them voice notes or texts of your poems, or meet up to write together. I did this with one of my best friends and fellow poets, it fostered a beautiful connection between us and we co-founded a collaborative poetry collective called Tandem Poets.

If you feel inspired by a particular prompt and want to write longer than 10 minutes or end up with two poems, bend the rules if it serves your writing, which is the most important thing. If the opposite happens, it's okay to have a mind blank or a rest. I even had people write one poem using two prompts. If you miss a week, resist punishing yourself by never starting again. You still deserve this, you're still a writer.

We will get to the writing soon, but I must tell you the main element that carried me to the 365th poem. It's unique to each of us and the fertiliser for everything we need to grow a healthy and abundant writing habit.

Why?

"He who has a why to live, can bear almost any how." – Friedrich Nietzsche

You may not be clear on your 'why' before you begin this journey but don't despair, it lives within your subconscious and still holds power. It may emerge from the depths of your soul on day 352 or decades after reading this book, but it is the reason you'll look back on this year at a growing body of work.

I encourage you to write a list of reasons why you want to write. It could be to try something new, have fun, or publish a poetry collection. After you've done this, I invite you to go deeper. Your 'why' will be what is driving that list. Perhaps it is to share your truth with the world or spend more time with your family. This 'why' helped you overcome the battles needed to get you here, and it will carry you through to the end.

My why is driven by love. A love for you and my seven year old self who wrote C.S Lewis's *The Lion the Witch and the Wardrobe* out on lined paper simply because she loved how writing felt. By writing this book, that love becomes tangible. Seeing *words in a book* isn't what gets me up in the morning but helping others to feel seen does. May this love reach you wherever you are and become your fertile field. Plant what you can and watch your words blossom.

Ready?

DAY 1: SHELL

Remember when we tried to make a meal
out of eggshells before we knew all they held?

Eggshells that cracked under light touch
and filled the morning with sunshine and clouds.

Two delicious dreams solidifying before our very eyes
when all we could imagine were two eggshells.

DAY 2: FIELD

Wisdom is a wildflower,
pick one and try to name it,

the flower dies, and another
waves from the next field.

Wisdom is the dip in the M
where two hills kiss in the distance,

draw near and the path bends
with only a moment to rest

before it's time to lift our gaze,
wander on,

questions riding on the soles of our feet,
no answers to stop and pick,

just the scent of wildflowers
on our fingertips.

DAY 3: TAKE

Take these feet, run to them
Take these hands, hold them
Take these arms, lift them
Take this heart, love them
Take these lips, tell them
Take these hips, carry them
Take this soul, save them.

DAY 4: WISH

A whisper through a window,
their face on the inside of your eyelids,
the name of that city now everywhere you look,
that ache in the crook of your neck,
the length of a deep sigh,
a glance at the clouds before the coffee run.
Sometimes the elephant in the room
but mostly the brief clarity of birdsong
from beyond the edges of your life
before the day moves on.

DAY 5: ONCE

Once upon a time, a story saved a life
do you remember the one that saved yours?

Once upon a time, a page turned over
do you remember holding your breath?

Once upon a time, a story ended
do you remember the stroke of sorrow?

Once upon a time, a new story began
do you remember the hope for tomorrow?

DAY 6: DOUBT

A flicker of doubt,
A tremble in a hand,
A shake in the voice,
A falter in a step,

A dark thought,
A closing throat,
A sob in a heart,
A shallow breath.

It's all just a flicker,
not an avalanche
hurricane,
or fence.

DAY 7: HARD

If I took you in a time machine
to the new shoots of my life,
if you saw what I've seen,
you would not believe this smile,
these wide eyes full of wonder,
this heart of mine eager to love.
There is revolution in my blood,
daisies pushing through the dirt
fully bloomed. There's no point
telling you I've had a hard life.
What does it matter?
I am a softly sprung daisy,
is that not enough?

DAY 8: INSIDE

Look at your shadow
out in the world, the one now dancing,
as you turn your back to the light.
Make it as big and small as you can,
call a friend to add theirs, make a peace sign,
move on until it waves *hello again*
from another patch of light.

Now do the same with your shadows
on the inside.

DAY 9: MEET

If I could go back to the beginning
and meet you again,

the limited times
I could reach for your hand

would not have begun
and I'd never reach again.

I'd walk so slowly
along the carpet of hours,

making sure you were always
one step ahead.

DAY 10: BREAKFAST

Today is a treasure, a gift,
outside in the gentle breeze
the melodic lilt of Spanish tongues
sing 'Buenos dias guappa!'
to their families and friends.

Their clothes are white,
they've come from mass,
and they float like angels or doves
to white plastic tables for the sweet nectar
of coffee and Churros.

I sit inside the vibrating drum
and wait for the breakfast
of the gods to land.
Today is a treasure, a gift,
and I plan to devour it all.

DAY 11: TOMORROW

Tiny is only tiny
from the perspective of today.

Tomorrow a drop grows into a puddle,
a puddle becomes a stream,
a stream flows into a river,
and a river feeds the ocean.

Tomorrow is a hobby, a month is practice,
six months a habit, a year, a skill,
five years a business, ten, expertise,
thirty, wisdom, and sixty, a legacy.

In sixty-one years,
we discover a new tiny,
and must become a drop
in the ocean of tomorrow.

DAY 12: FAITH

I have to believe
that we can come back from this
and not base my happiness on whether we do
because that will look like judgment to you
and why should you carry that?

I have to believe
that we can come back from this,
even if it means giving up hope
of who we are or will become.
Worthiness is beyond what I can believe,
so I call Faith and ask her to run.

DAY 13: MANIFEST

I wrote on moths,
moths appeared.

I sang my love,
love knocked.

I danced in shadows,
darkness swirled.

I made a sign,
the way arrived.

DAY 14: CARE

What thoughts can I gift you today,
that will lift you from your heaviness?
Tell me and I will write them into the world,
and hang them on the trees along your daily walk
for you to pass and revisit, again and again.
You'll catch yourself singing like a bird,
I care, for you, for you,
that is how I'd like them to be heard.

DAY 15: HANDS

Hands wipe a brow,
to cool a burning head.

Hands stir the pot,
to feed a hungry belly.

Hands write a letter,
to soothe a heavy heart.

Hands sew cloth,
to warm cold shoulders.

Hands wipe tears,
to comfort all sorrows.

Hands stretch high,
to celebrate your wins.

Hands scrub skin,
to cleanse life's grime.

Hands patch knees,
to heal life's wounds.

Where hands work,
a prayer is in the room.

DAY 16: EXPLAIN

How do you explain
everything a mother is,

and begin to pay her back
for the hours, the tears, the skin?

A butterfly does not spend its life
thanking the cocoon,

I'm pretty sure it disintegrates,
so there is nothing to thank

but I try to as it dawns on me
all that a mother is and has to be,

all that she was and had to be,
for me to be all that I can.

DAY 17: JAM

In this house, there's a love note laboratory,
memory depository and nostalgia factory.

In this house, there's a conversation starter,
a taste taverna and time decanter.

In this house, there's an Alladin's Lamp
full of pops, nan and gramps.

In this house there's a magic wellspring,
filling busy breakfasts and lazy lunches.

In this house tiny hands try to reach
the treasure, and the answer is always yes,

the lid is always loosened, bellies bulging
with life's simple goodness.

DAY 18: IMPERFECT

It's okay to make the wrong choice.
Trying to reason with, beautify, or fix
a wrong choice and turn it into a lesson
isn't what empties our bodies of shame,
people, our people, love us through all choices,
there's room for both wrong *and* right,
in a perfectly imperfect life.

DAY 19: SLOW

To the slow coach, slowpoke and faffer,
loiterer, dilly-dallier and daydreamer,

did you know the Corpus Christi Clock
is only on time once every five minutes?

If a clock in Cambridge can be late for itself,
next time a speedy mac-reedy tuts

when you're late for a race
only they want to run, tell them:

Did you know the Corpus Christi Clock
is only on time once every five minutes?

DAY 20: SOFT

I always thought the best type of people
were hammers, and then I met a cushion.

At first, I just stared, expecting it to reveal spikes,
I prodded it hard, it went all the way in

and sprang back like Winnie the Pooh's
soft bulging belly, then nothing happened.

I said sorry and waited for the blow,
but it asked if I needed a hug.

I cried yes, it got wet, and stayed
until the tears soaked in, forever gone.

For the rest of my days,
I forgot what a hammer was.

DAY 21: WEIGHT

Remember how good it feels to be dead weight,
limbs spread out like a starfish?

They say we should tread lightly around the earth
but how do we avoid becoming ghosts?

I know I'm alive when my hip catches
the corner of a table or another's universe,

or when the press on my limbs linger,
marked by weighty meat and skin.

Where are you substance? Who will trade
feather light for plentiful?

Am I forever destined to be an ark,
and never the animal?

DAY 22: TWIN

For every person who judges,
there is a person who accepts.

For every person who drags,
there is a person who lifts.

For every person who hurts,
there is a person who heals.

For every person who leaves,
there is a person who stays.

For every person who hates,
there is a person who loves.

For every person alone,
   there is *us*.

DAY 23: DESIGN

I stand across from you
and see an entire universe,

I stare for so long, that I no longer know
which is truth and which is reflection.

Does a flower know what colour its petals will grow
before it sees its own kind in a meadow?

Does a flower know it is a flower
because we named it so?

DAY 24: MEAL

If this is the meat of my life, it's the prime cut.
Everything I couldn't stomach once has returned
to feed me now that there is room enough.
I want to get on my knees and kiss the earth,
thank the tough morsels of years, thin pickings
full of soggy lettuce hearts, rotten potatoes
and half-arsed vegetables that never grew big enough.
Now I know how it feels to be full, and life is juicy,
well-seasoned and tender, sliding off the bone.

DAY 25: LONELY

If the first breath you take this morning,
whispers, *hello lonely*,

take yourself to a café,
and practice asking for what you want.

Order once, twice, or more,
the owner will be happy to see you,

the coffee will be smooth, the toast,
buttery and delicious.

They'll ask for your name and you'll say,
I'm lonely, and when you ask for the bill,

they'll tell you to put your purse away,
and your heart will race, wondering why.

They'll disappear amongst trays and plates,
and return with the bill. It'll read: Your smile already paid.

You'll catch your reflection in the café window,
and collect the change.

DAY 26: DUST

I spin on the axis of impermanence,
that stills its tumble

when your hand above my head
becomes home.

I sweep dust with a swirl,
melodies laugh from our mouths,

high on the fact that
we both know the sounds.

Our awkward edges
try to feel for the future,

you lead, I follow, you rise
and I fall in just one spin,

and for a moment,
worry is a wallflower,

watching us dance
till the end of our days.

DAY 27: HOW

How do I talk of wings and not the angels,
butterflies and doves?

How do I sing of wings and not hum
the beat, soar and flight?

How do I write of wings and not ink
your name on every line?

How do I dream of wings and not watch
us rise from old and tired lives?

DAY 28: ORDER

We order people onto our plates and our eyes
can be bigger than our bellies.

There's always a price to pay, it's a gamble
to find new and delicious ways to be satisfied,

so next time you peruse, remember:
receiving what you want from life

is as simple as ordering from a menu.

Don't allow others to order for you
or rush your options to please other hungry people.

Take it from someone who loves to eat,
choose wisely and chew slowly.

DAY 29: SACRED

We made a sacred promise
but I forget what it was,

I only know how it felt,
my pinky in yours.

I've wandered down
the corridors of our days

exploring each room
for what it contained,

but all I hear are the words,
I promise

a promise we wrote,
a promise that lives,

a promise I know,
we wanted to keep.

DAY 30: CLOUD

Hope
   is a passing cloud.

DAY 31: CONFESS

P.S. Are you ready to hear everything I meant to say,
before I shut the door faster than I wanted to
as if tomorrow I'd have another chance?
Are you sitting down?
Oh! Hang on, someone is at the door,
don't go anywhere.

Dad?

DAY 32: CONTENTS

We trust a clasp until it breaks,
pretending it still works for longer than we should,
struggling not to spill out the contents of our lives,
balancing and rebalancing the weight of all we hold.

What are we afraid to see scattered across the street?
Have you dared to look? Or do you throw the broken box
into the dustbin and walk away as if it doesn't belong to you?
Never seeing what you fought so hard to keep.

DAY 33: LIFELINE

I've never told anyone this before,
but the lifeline on my left hand
branches out into two different paths,
and I think you should know.

I've measured which line is longer (the left),
and scoured them for clues to pinpoint
when the fracture may arrive,
but it could have already passed.

Am I going to get sick?

If you knew which path led to the longest life,
wouldn't you? How can I choose
when I only see its length
and not its laughter?

DAY 34: LINK

We were
never made
to be the end
of all things
but the link
through which
all things
are carried
to the end.

DAY 35: AFTER

After,
the sky sheds
tears on my skin.
We're mid-heatwave,
but the cloud arrives
and wants to speak.

I search for meaning,
but all I can think is,
*why are things harder
after healing?*

DAY 36: BEES

I spy them
weaving unfalteringly
at the centre of the hum,
one eye on this conversation,
the other on the next one.

Five strong, no words,
just a nod or glance,
like a team of athletes
with one mind,
indomitable sisters
made so only how
a diamond is formed.

Queen Bees.

In this hive,
no one is left behind.
I see one lose her wing,
a world of pain present,
I swoop in steady and lift.
Her wing is mine.
We are the hive,
and we dance Sevillanas,

then Rumba and dissolve
into a sway of hips and hands,
enjoying the world
we keep turning,
from the inside,
before we return
to our work.

DAY 37: BUBBLES

Where do they pop off to?
Is there a place
they've always
dreamed of seeing?

One day,
I'll float beyond
the sky's edge,
and understand
why it was meant to be
a surprise.

DAY 38: RUN

I hope you are okay.
I woke in the dead of night
and wanted to call you
but you might've been sleeping,
I hoped you were sleeping.
I mean to say
I hoped you'd not
I hope you are okay
I mean to say I need you,
I mean to say I'm scared, too,
as in it's okay to *want to*
as in I hope you know, *I know, too,*
as in, call me, and I will run.

DAY 39: FUNCTION

We try hard to beautify that which
no longer has a function,

like gold paint on a cracked plate,
like a mosaic, like our bodies,

like this Well.

We plant flowers around and tell
children that if they throw gold coins

and are respectful,
the Well will grant wishes,

like the elderly dishing out sweets
from the deep pockets of time.

Why can't a Well be a Well
that is alright as itself?

DAY 40: WORRY

There is no worry carried past
a good night's sleep
and the dawn chorus in Palma Del Rio
reminds me, I love mornings.
The impulse to return to work softens,
I become one with the sounds,
before these orange trees become
a forgotten shade of green,
and my presence here, an absence.
I dance in these streets
as if tomorrow will never come
because life's alarm is about to ring,
and soon I must wake up.

DAY 41: HAIR

My dog has shed herself
over every pillow, sheet,
floor, and t-shirt I've owned.

She's licked her private parts
in front of new flames
and barked at new friends
I tried to make.

But I've stopped picking
her hair off my body
with a heavy sigh because
there will come a day

when her bark is silent,
her final hair will shed,
and I'll spend my grief
collecting them.

DAY 42: PHOTOGRAPH

A beautiful pause
hung up on the wall
to stare at relentlessly
when reality shows us little
of what we're looking for.

DAY 43: CHAMPION

If it wasn't weird to fan you in public
while your chin stuck out proud
like the deity you are, I would.
I'd even feed you grapes –
unless you were allergic,
that would be awkward
but I'd find another way
to give you a sweet taste.
It would be succulent,
embarrassingly inadequate,
but I'd attempt it all the same.
That is how I like to fan –
spread out wide, audible
and in your face.

DAY 44: STICK

I've always dreaded this game.
The children would cackle,
wrench the stick from my hand
and show me how to do it 'properly'.
Even now, it makes me nauseous
to see a crazed mob take turns
beating sweets out of an unarmed thing
while everyone cheers and claps.

So what if Mary-Jane looks adorable?
I think of nothing but lynching.
I always knew trees weren't made
for hanging or hitting and neither was I.

DAY 45: OPPORTUNITY

Go out and meet her
in an open field,

she'll be so glad to see you,
you've not visited for so long

and the grass has almost forgotten
the press of your footprint.

Go today,
and tell us what you find.

DAY 46: LIMITS

A patch of light waits
on the other side of the shade
for you to forget
where you have placed
your limits.

As your skin begins to burn,
you know you must go
or become ash.

DAY 47: PRISON

Whatever bars you're looking through,

turn around - now they are behind you.

Put one foot in front of the other until

there's enough space to swing your arms.

Take another step, forget what bars are

and how cold they felt against your face.

Fill your lungs with oxygen, and release.

Did you know, that only you can do that?

DAY 48: SMILE

We've been at war with teeth for too long,
from teething tantrums to tooth fairy exploitation,
wobbling, pushing and thumping with a tongue,

forcing those who dare to make their own way,
back in line, scouring them until they cry red tears,
drowning them in coffee and red wine.

We curse them when they age, replacing them
for younger models, mourning our faces,
not their graves when they die.

But what about the time they saved your life
when a sharp tooth was the only weapon
you knew how to use?

DAY 49: TOXIC

You try to build a bridge towards my body again,
I see you coming, and do not hide this time.
I wonder if you're a strong swimmer.
If you die out there, I will be blamed,
even though you're the one who jumped,
because we bridges are told
we must be grateful for the footfall
but have you seen what they've done to us?
So even though my hands shake,
I pick up the pieces and build another bridge
    towards myself
as your jaw drops into the stream.

DAY 50: MIDNIGHT

Had I known a lizard
would have darted its way into my life at midnight,
bringing you with it, I would have kept the door open.

As we laughed, squealed, poked and prodded
the fugitive away into the night, something else crept in
before I had time to close the backdoor.

I was tempted to invite the lizard back and ask him
if our soft bodies fit together like sleeping cubs
because of the late hour or something worth opening

all future doors for. He would have told me,
but I was scared and let him go.

DAY 51: PERMISSION

I wrote you a poem
I wrote you a poem
stop scrolling
I wrote you a poem
you are ready
you are ready
you are ready
you are ready
for the thing
you think you need
permission for
you are ready
you are already
ready to do that thing
or be that someone.

DAY 52: ROLLER-COASTER

Remember the loop de loop?
The name for all roller-coasters
that made your stomach flip just by looking at it.

I remember yellow, screams and cheers,
Southend Pier, and the sea opening its mouth
to swallow whoever fell.

I tried to differentiate between
the screams and cheers, in any case,
no one could get off before it was time.

I wonder where those people are now,
and if they know of their bravery,
choosing to get on even though
it might've made them sick.

DAY 53: DOOR

A key doesn't always look like one.
Sometimes, the key is to walk in the opposite direction
of the one you've been walking in for months,
arrive at a sunflower field you never knew was there
in a part of town that never existed before,
and watch what opens.

DAY 54: ENGLISH

When we have news, the English
like to pop the kettle on, gather the troops,
take out a cup, tea bag, milk and spoon,
one foot leaning on the other at the place
where silence begins to boil before
the news spills out after a few false starts.

This time, I'm alone. I want to celebrate
with friends and wine, but I also want
to swirl the spoon, hold the news in my hands,
quench my thirst with something warm,
curl up on the sofa with Mum, dunk a biscuit,
    and disappear into a quiet hug.

DAY 55: HOT

The hottest thing
to enter and leave the mouth

is a healthy conversation
at the most inconvenient time,

maybe halfway
through something else.

You'll never feel so aroused,
a single sheet encasing your world,

naked from soul to toe
wrapped in the knowledge

that care is more important
than crave, and lovability

isn't a pre-requisite
to pleasing the crowd.

In the end, it's not about
getting hot,

too much spice and the
hungry tongue goes numb,

you don't have to set yourself on fire
   to be loved.

DAY 56: DISTANCE

An arm span is all there is
to bridge the unfathomable distance
between two lovers together and alone
in the same thing.

DAY 57: CLAP

If Music were a country,
its Capital would be Andalucia,
It's people, my favourite song,
each day, an exquisite melody
drawing Duende out of me.
The hum of La Feria delivering
love notes from hands to feet,
reawakening sleeping body parts,
a cacophony of sounds and shouts,
led by the drum of our hearts,
body and soul as one,
dance, clap, sing, repeat
and the beat goes on, and on.

DAY 58: GUESS

It speaks in every language,
skips to the click of the kettle,
settles on a stare longer than a blink,
and sits on a sigh for five more minutes.

It shapes its name on exposed skin,
snuggles in the silence of a darkened room
and sings its own vowels in the shower.

So clear – when it appears,
that you never need to call it,
it's so significantly there
     when it is.

DAY 59: MINE

The first kitchen I could dance in,
wearing nothing but nail polish.

The first lounge I did not have to rush through
to avoid unwanted conversation.

The first bedroom with no need to cover my mouth
so screams or sobs wouldn't be heard.

The first second bedroom I could make up a use for
and change without a reason.

The first bathroom stress could soak in for hours
with the water filled up to the rim.

The first garden to nurture my overflowing life
so I could speak openly with the stars.

The first home I did not need to share but would have
if you'd asked.

DAY 60: GHOST

You have a visitor.
They're at your door now,
they don't need to knock or ring the bell,
you can sense they're there.

Open the door,
do not rush to fill the space
just stand there and take them in.
It's been so long and yet
perhaps a few seconds,
notice how their hair sits,
the shape of their mouth,
the message in their eyes
that says I will not leave
unless you ask me to.
Open your mouth,
and tell them *everything*.

You might need hours
or just a few seconds
and they'll say, I know, I know
that's why I'm here,
but I was waiting until
you saw me so clearly at your door

that I couldn't not be...

When there is nothing left to say,
ask them to leave, close the door,
pick a sock up off the floor,
wash a plate or two, no one
need ever know except for you
and your ghost.

DAY 61: DIRECTION

The greatest advice I've ever received
came from my driving instructor:
Wherever your gaze, there you'll go.
If you're looking at the houses,
the pedestrians, the trees,
or the road you missed,
you'll veer in that direction.

Focus on the road in front of you,
not too far, not too close, follow the line,
and you will never stray from your lane.
You'll get to where you want to go.

DAY 62: WOUND

I scraped my elbow,
I've no idea how or when,

I tried to squeeze it for ideas
but it won't tell me, it cries out instead.

Perhaps it doesn't know how or when,
but that one day there was no pain,

and now there is, and that's all
it will ever feel.

We don't notice we're walking
wounds around the earth,

while our skin tries to heal,
with nothing but sun and time.

DAY 63: CREDITS

Moving to Spain was a movie,
and now the credits are rolling in
over the plains of Sevilla province.
All subtext and meaning crescendo
to what will soon be a black screen.

Do protagonists know when the end credits
are about to roll because everything hangs
under a musical sky that doesn't know
how to do anything else but build?

A short time ago, everything felt
like it could only ever be a beginning
and now endings shoot up everywhere,
as I run minimising toward the backdrop.

It feels radical. To love endings.
We should give them more credit.
They rarely get the applause they deserve,
all they've ever wanted is for us
not to need them anymore.

DAY 64: TODAY

Today I say yes to no
   yes to right,
   yes to slow,
   yes to, I don't know right now
   but I'm here figuring it out.

Today I say yes
   to the me of my dreams
   to that dream that's always felt
   like a no because a yes means...
   more yeses.

Yes
   is the most powerful word there is,
   it's the womb of all other words
   and all other worlds.

I move from yes
   I breathe from yes
   existence here
   on this planet is a yes,
   and I live that yes
   I am that yes.

DAY 65: MISSION

We have one life
and the mission is to
decrease the proximity
between you and
what you perceive
as not you.

DAY 66: FATE

I hold the Acceptance de Destino in my hands,
which mistranslates to Acceptance of Fate, which means
the anchor has dropped and will hold me to account.
It's too late to think about all that could've been
but that doesn't stop the flood coming in.
It's my fault for being swept out to sea,
   I might as well let it carry me.

DAY 67: LIST

A list of things we do and say to avoid saying
- I'm sad

- Shut up
- I'm fine
- I'm tired
- I've got so much to do
- I'm really busy
- you must have lots to do
- I should eat/shower/work/leave
- bye then
- see you around
- I'm not feeling well
- whatever
- do want you want
- I don't mind
- I hate you
- avoiding eye contact
- posting on Instagram
- cleaning the house
- making no plans
- making too many plans
- pretending that person is the last person you want to see
- sending them funny Instagram reels to make them smile

- making jokes to their face at their expense
- overachieving
- disappearing off the face of the earth
- being annoyed at your friends when they don't follow
- oversharing to a stranger, hoping they say it before you don't

DAY 68: STILL

You can melt
and still have substance

you can burn
and still shine bright

you can give light
and still cast a shadow

emit heat
and still feel the cold night.

You can strike a match
and still get snuffed out

alight another,
still keep a flame for yourself

You can use a stick
and still cast a spell,

you can melt
and still, and still...

DAY 69: LOOK

Look for a sign
and my computer crashes.
I can't do anything but tell you
it might have been a sign
but sometimes a sign isn't
what actually happens,
it's how we feel when we're close
to the sign we're looking for,
even if it doesn't have a shape
and can't be touched,
the things we want to see
are signs enough,
and can bring a person home
to whatever joy there is in this life
   even if we can't stay there forever.

DAY 70: FEAR

There is no fear
like the fear

that your breath
is about to fail you,

but over time,
like with most parents,

we can forgive fallibility
and remember,

though it falters
a few times,

it doesn't give up
for a million other moments.

DAY 71: IMPACT

If you do not want to shatter,
be like water
let any hard thing that hits you take the impact.
Choose not to drown whatever sinks,
who wants a graveyard scattered along their bed?
Not all trinkets become treasure with age,
fish will die trying to make homes out of them.
So be like water, watch all that enters
float to the surface, towards the shore,
and out of your body forever.

DAY 72: SPEAK

All the things you've never said,
  have never left.

DAY 73: CHAIN

Those who've had to twist most in this life
become springs.

Have you ever tried to snap a spring?
It's like biting into a chain.

DAY 74: STRANGE

We are unloved in places
we fight so hard to be loved.

We are loved in the places
we feel most unlovable.

We travel to the places
we know the most about.

We never travel to places
we can't spell.

DAY 75: SECRET

There is no point telling you what I know,
what I can see through, what you think is opaque,
whilst spending your life trying to be an anomaly
who only knows the answer to yourself.

I see stories in your silence and noise in your novels,
so when you return to make up for something
no one is holding against you, I'll close my eyes
and pretend your homecoming is the greatest surprise,

and it really will be so lovely to see you
try and make it all about me.

DAY 76: DARKNESS

There is so much to see,
what is it that you're scared to find,
and do you dare to meet it?

DAY 77: DESERVE

Did you know Hermit crabs
line up in size order alongside vacant shells
and the best fit gets to move in?

We arrive at a small mansion,
and my landlady tells me ten people
own this house on a teacher's wage.

I'm wondering why I've been invited,
but I soon see what a family can be,
not something to survive, or fight,

but something to be a part of,
a reason to try and people
to rise alongside.

So even if I'm a Hermit crab, forever
trying on shells for size amongst those
who often forget they're Hermit crabs,

I'm still part of the beach,
I still deserve to call a shell Home,
and one day it will be my turn to fit.

DAY 78: GOOGLE

Type the word *Stranded* into Google,
and images of serene beaches appear,
with empty deck chairs placed under
a single palm tree facing the still ocean.

There are no images of narrow eyes,
a shrug of deliberate ignorance,
a stare that runs ice-cold through you
from someone above their pay grade.

There are no videos of the word no, or worse,
I don't know, in a place full of people
who do not see you as anything more than
an obstruction to manoeuvre around.

I never saw a serene beach in the refugee camps,
or a still ocean in the eyes of the boy
who followed us around a detention centre
in case we had space for him in our camera bag.

There were no deck chairs, just a stolen mattress
that volunteers squeezed through a gap in a fence
so a newborn would not begin their life
with their face in the dirt.

Stranded is a war zone, the last flight gone,
an unknown street in a foreign smoggy city,
a dark underground car park,
the space between a wall and a gun.

Stranded is not a beach, it is to melt into the walls
unable to speak of or touch the things that once said,
I am, that once said,
I am free,
that once said,
I'll never let anyone harm my children.

DAY 79: SLEEP

I slip between its folds into a new day
   that does not have you in it.

DAY 80: RESCUE

I wave and smile at passersby.
From this distance, I look like I'm climbing
but I'm just falling upward ever so slowly,

I hope no one notices, I hope someone does,
I hope someone reads SOS in my smile
and rescues me, even if I assure them,

I'm fine, I'm fine!
Please help me.

The passersby are still waving – are you okay?
Hang on in there, I'm coming to you!

DAY 81: DUCK

Little duck,
you've been treading water for so long

you absolutely can
do this all on your own

but know,
you don't have to

and that sinking
gives another

the chance to swim.
Little duck,

falling into their soft care
allows them

the opportunity to rise,
and meet their strength.

So if you can't do it for you
little duck, do it for them.

DAY 82: FAVOURITE

I savour each adoration as they unfurl
like the pink-tinged rose petals you nuzzle your nose in.

I wish I could speak of my own country
as if it were the scent of a flower or a long-lost lover.

DAY 83: ACCIDENT

After 20 years, I'm finally here. Albeit by accident,
or mistake, at least not how I imagined.

It's all so *Paris*, diluted yet simmering,
sensual, yet no one is touching each other.

I scour the streets searching for signs of romance,
attempting to eke it out amongst traffic and smog.

Two men try to kiss each other goodbye at the metro,
but their heads turn so far away from each other,

they kiss the backs of each other's heads.
One gives the other a brown paper bag

and tries to leave still holding it, the other
takes the bag while pushing it further away,

It's all so - *Paris*.

DAY 84: CORNER

Is it the obstacle,
or the anti-space?

DAY 85: CHANGE

After the best decision has been made,
the dream followed, the whisper listened to,
the leap of faith well and truly leaped,
what are we to do then?

DAY 86: LAY

Lay in a non-descript field
between Paris and Calais
and let the grass absorb time.

The earth will work on you
and you'll grow so green here
and renew every Spring.

Lay long enough to let flowers
grow from your hands so the bees
will know where to rest.

DAY 87: STUCK

London is a greenhouse of self-contained plants,
growing only so far in too small pots.
They're sprayed with graffiti to make struggle beautiful,
and placed under synthetic light to make them do things
that plants weren't designed to do.

There is no direct sunlight behind the office blocks,
just chewing gum rain on pavements, and forced smiles,
I try to love where I was born, but it's no use,
I'm a native flower gone rogue, a weed,
trying to pull itself out from the root.

DAY 88: REACH

There is no reaching you here,
everything the tired light touches was designed
to keep us from looking each other in the eye.

DAY 89: ART

Méson La Muralla,
Salmorejo in the welcome heat –
Gambas al ajillo con pan,
children playing in the park
below the mauve sky
as the evening dons a shawl of stars,
and the ancient city wall
becomes shadow and dust.

There is no need to learn
Lorca's plays or read his poetry
to travel to the *Jardin de Andalucia,*
take my hand and we'll live within the art,
as the poems he would've written
if he'd had just a little more time.

DAY 90: MEMORY

In someone else's life, parts of us
have been moved to a folder
we haven't the power to name.

We're nothing but storage space,
irretrievable with immediacy –
never to be accidentally stumbled on again.

It's not the immediacy we miss,
but the intimacy that will cause us
to relive memories long after

we should've deleted them to make space
for new ones, believing our love belonged
in some shared cloud.

DAY 91: HUG

There is no holding her for more than ten seconds,
I tell her it takes twenty seconds for dopamine to release,
five seconds in, she's shaking, ten seconds, gone.

I pull her back and give her the hug I need,
and have needed for the past thirty years.

Tears arrive on the shoreline but never leave the port
before she tries to hold back the sea again. I tell myself
it's the intimacy she can't bear.

DAY 92: BLUSH

Andalucian Blush: the sign of a day well and truly kissed
and *oh* how I kiss her and hope to every night.

DAY 93: BRUNCH

Languid and sleepy, with a half-smile
and slight coffee breath,

enough time to make good choices
and not have to begin them yet,
a promise to call family, later,
make extravagant plans,
or even better – nap.

May there always be Brunch,
a dream of all the things we *could* do,

but that which we gloriously don't *have* to
until well after lunch.

DAY 94: BUILD

All I know is that
one step at a time
around the world
does not leave footprints
in a straight line
and staying
on the same course
keeps what is
as it always was.

DAY 95: LIVING

It is what our days are for.

DAY 96: FACE

My friends respond to my reels
but not my calls or check-in texts.

They flick through my stories
but do not have time to listen to them.

Remember our heads tilted close
over coffee, eyes glistening

as if we were the only two people
in the world?

Now I share you with strangers,
who will never haul you back up

from the public toilet floor
to wipe the snot from your face.

I steal other people's art online
to tell you I miss your smile

and do not credit them
for saying the things I can't quite.

DAY 97: LONGING

Putting bait at the end of a hook
and throwing a line into a stream
where I know fish do not swim.

DAY 98: ANT

Interdependency
  is strength

just look at the forests
  the bees, the ants.

DAY 99: GO

Go to the water
   surrender this night

wherever you like,
   no matter its size –

ocean, stream,
   bathtub, eyes,

Go to the water
   and surrender this night.

Go to the water
   today or tonight

wash off the day
   make yourself light.

DAY 100: ALONE

I've only had three hours of sleep
and my solid green boots
have abandoned me.

We left on bad terms –
they didn't want to leave Spain
and so they walked away from me
and my heavy feet that drag them
in directions they're too old to roam.

It's for the best,
but I never told them that,
I said I'd be happier alone.

DAY 101: GROW

I heard someone say
they were disappointed
with the wildflowers this year.

How can a wildflower
be anything other than
tenacious, resilient, and rare?

I worried they were disappointed
in me too, and then I remembered
I was a Wildflower

- too busy growing to care.

DAY 102: LEFT

There is an impression of me
that lives in a memory foam mattress

at a flat I no longer rent.

For the past eight months,
I've melted into it

making a shape out of habit,
and now a new tenant

whose face I will never see,
and whose body I will never hold

will know every inch of me,
and where I reached out to

in the dark secret nights,
where only terrors should be,

longer than good lovers
have left impressions on me.

A Note on Themed Prompts

Hello! I want to say a huge well done for getting this far, you may have written nothing short of 100 poems by now and if you haven't done so already, give yourself a huge pat on the back.

This is a brief introduction to the themed prompts. Not only are themes a great way to unlock your imagination and get the pen flowing, but themed submission call-outs are common amongst poetry presses, competitions, and magazines.

If you're putting together a pamphlet or chapbook*, want to apply to the Ginkgo Poetry Prize**, or are interested in writing about a niche topic, these themed prompts will give you a head-start. You may even want to submit them after some editing.

There are 29 themes for you to work your way through and they increase in size. For example, you will write on the same theme with different daily prompts for a week, and then monthly. This can support any projects you are working towards or help you create new material.

Now would be a good time to return to the 'How to Keep Going' chapter and re-familiarise yourself. This will help you from here on out. Then write down a few thoughts about your journey so far, what have you discovered?

In case you've forgotten, you're doing the best you can and I'm so proud of you. I'd love to hear how you get on with the themed prompts, happy writing!

*A small collection of poems, typically no more than 24 poems or 50 pages.

**A major international award for eco-poetry.

THEME: NATURE

I believe a leaf of grass is no less than the journey-work of the stars.

Walt Whitman

DAY 103: TREES

Grace our shade and rest,
lay on the grass and watch us
dance with the life you too have inside
and marvel at your own making.

DAY 104: BUD

I always thought
your hands were beautiful,
and I watched them intently
as you softly strummed the guitar.

After all these years, I still remember
how gently you plucked the strings
as if you cared for them too much
to fully touch them,

the same tenderness you showed
when you stroked my cheek.

DAY 105: ROOST

You can arrive at a place
that you have no recollection
of leaving, living in, or being formed
and still know - you've come home.

DAY 106: RAINBOW

Rainbows are dreams
   trying to find a place to land.

DAY 107: GRAVITY

You can ride this wave,
do you want to know why?

You're not just the swimmer,
the wave, or the Ocean,

you are the Moon,
moving the tide.

DAY 108: MOUNTAIN

(Where is everyone?)

When
you've teetered
for so long on the edge
just to prove you can, you start
to forget why you climbed so far from
everyone and everything else to get to the top.

DAY 109: STORM

I'm writing this poem
thousands of feet in the air

as we're flung through turbulence,
bouncing between clouds.

The children are starting to cry,
and the quiet passengers guffaw

in sharp bursts when the plane dives,
so I'll say it, I love you with all my heart.

I can love you only with my heart,
and perhaps never again with words.

I know you'll think I'm being dramatic,
that is unless this storm wins,

in which case, this will be another
silence in the quickening of your days,

which I hope are full of joy
and sex, and by that I mean,

anything that the world
thinks you should enjoy

behind closed doors,
like where I might be going now.

THEME: COLOURS

*Mere colour, unspoiled by meaning, and unallied
with definite form, can speak to the soul in a thousand different ways.*

Oscar Wilde

DAY 110: PURPLE

What is my favourite colour,
if it isn't yours?

I was gifted a purple
friendship bracelet

because I spent
so much time touching it,

wondering how
I could fill your life up

with all that you loved,
the shopkeeper

thought I was in love
with the bracelet.

DAY 111: BLUE

I lie on the blue carpet and wait
for my past to sail in like a fleet of ships

as the door swings,
hoping I may dance with it.

I'm a tiny limbed baby fleshy squid
bobbing along the rapids at Butlins.

I almost drown because no one
is strong enough to pull me out.

After the fourth ride, I'm plucked out
by the hair – like an underwater turnip.

I'm back on the blue carpet and watch
the sun kiss the single tree outside,

the leaves blush, and I avert my eyes.
I won't witness the seasons change her.

DAY 112: ORANGE

There is a saying in Palma Del Rio,
encontrar tu media naranja
(to find your half orange),
it's equivalent to a soul mate
or twin flame and you'll know
when you've found yours.

I found mine, yes,
the love of my life and no,
it's not a person, but, *a people*,
a people that love me more than
everything I ever had to lose to gain.

DAY 113: GOLD

I've never cared
for the value of Gold,

I pretend to - catch myself
talking about buying

and selling, all the while
picturing golden light

glistening off the skin
of spring water,

cupped hands collecting
its nectar towards my lips,

quenching my thirst
for everything.

DAY 114: WHITE

The fresh linen billows
in the soft breeze.

We air them out like sails
along the valley,

to welcome good things
into our lives like eggs,

and milk, lillies
and breath,

as ordinarily,
as getting dressed,

as often
as the first yawn.

DAY 115: GREY

Your stare, the closing of a gate
the end of an afternoon,
something cleansed
and not yet dry.

DAY 116: RED

Everyone on the train
clutches books.

One man has two,
one with an orange

on the front cover,
on the subject of home,

and a red book titled
Trespasses.

Louise is the authors
first name,

a bookmark pokes its head
out of the pages and reads,

you know.

THEME: FIRSTS

The beauty of any first time is that it leads to a thousand others.

Pico Iyer

DAY 117: KISS

Chlorine drips
from slippery limbs,
a grey lock clicks
in a blue sterile cubicle.
Our bodies brace
and find no edge
to push against,
no real pieces
of each other,
just a black hole
we both fall into
Unscathed.

DAY 118: HEARTBREAK

There is a ghost of a girl at the window,
her face could be mistaken for the moon.

There is a ghost of a girl at the window,
tell her I'm coming for her soon.

There is a ghost of a girl at the window,
her face could be mistaken for the moon.

There is a ghost of a girl at the window,
tell her I'm coming for her soon.

DAY 119: DREAM JOB

I tried to pre-empt its moods,
understand the lack of its shape,
and chased its shadow as if it were
a birthday or school crush.

I catapulted and cartwheeled
to where I hoped it would wait,
if I ran quickly enough, I'd catch it,
but I fell hard, and something else

came towards me, held out a hand,
pulled me up, and walked alongside me,
to the end of my days.

DAY 120: SUMMER FLING

Squelch an olive between your teeth,
float away on an ocean breeze
like the first time salt-licked your skin
in the Mediterranean. When shoulders sank,
toes wriggled into the sand under a heavy gaze,
and you bathed in a steady smile that stopped time.
Olives taste of that place just beyond the horizon -
a perfect day with the perfect person.

DAY 121: GETAWAY

Blanes, without a care in the world.
No one could steal us from that night,
even the sea threw back her head and laughed
as we giggled with our entire bodies,
hair whipping our cheeks to the tinkling
of chinking glasses. The sea, still laughing,
took a liking to me and washed up a wish,
like sand between my toes I've carried it since.
I tossed the wish back polished smooth over time,
and asked her to wash up another, which she did.

DAY 122: ARGUMENT

Our first friend
gifts us our first loss,
so honour their name
every time you find yourself
loss upon loss upon loss.

DAY 123: CHILD

Grief is the butterfly,
and love – the cocoon.

THEME: NUMBERS

Pure mathematics is, in its way, the poetry of logical ideas.

Albert Einstein

DAY 124: TWENTY-ONE

We know you want a surprise party,
but you're too scared to ask,

and yes you want a gift and no
you don't want to be alone,

and yes people should make a fuss and no
your bestie who lives abroad won't miss it

and yes we know you enough by now, and no,
we won't stop finding ways to celebrate you

in as many days and yes,
you do deserve it.

DAY 125: TWELVE

At twelve I left home
and half of me behind,

clothes shoved in bin bags,
a long car journey ride,

hope for safety slowly fading,
the longer we drove.

DAY 126: THIRTY-FOUR

People who loved you at thirty
may not at thirty-one.

A place you loved at thirty-two,
may be gone at thirty-three.

Wishes that come true at thirty-three
may bring woes at thirty-four

and woes that come at thirty-four,
may bring joy at thirty-five.

DAY 127: ONE

There are a hundred reasons not to write
and only one that means you must.

If that one reason sings in your heart,
then by all means – *you must.*

DAY 128: TWO

They say three is a magic number
but it never feels magic, just rational.

I prefer two odd-sized legs holding
the other up awkwardly, against all odds.

A tripod is so perfunctory,
that the legs don't even need to touch.

DAY 129: ELEVEN

Eleven was my favourite number to multiply.
I loved seeing the same clean number

like two dancers about to begin,
a rhythm I could keep up with.

I've been dancing with angels,
ever since.

DAY 130: THIRTEEN

I wish you the best of days,
the best of all days

and even on the days
that aren't the best,

I hope you can see they're
the best they're meant to be,

even if today's best
is meant to be

nothing but
a delicious mess.

THEME: MUSIC

Where words fail, music speaks.

Hans Christian Andersen

DAY 131: MELODY

When I leave this life
I'll return as music,

and be loved so much
by so many,

regardless of how
I present myself at the bar,

for all my strange
arrangements.

I will be the relief a man turns to
when his breath fails to sing.

I will matter that much,
and move that many,

I'll be the joyful whistle
when life is sweet,

and the melody that speaks
when words can only seek to wonder.

DAY 132: CHOIR

If we sang like a choir,
life would be beautiful.

If we listened like a choir,
war would cease.

If we socialised like a choir –
let's not talk about that one.

DAY 133: CRESCENDO

Allow what is, to be what is,
unless someone has their hands

around your neck, or your light
in which case, fight like an alley cat,

give them the fright of their lives
by loving your peace *so hard*.

DAY 134: SOUNDTRACK

What's yours?
I try to think of mine,
more tired than I've ever been,
hurtling through the grey
with the occasional glimpse
of the green river Thames,
Spotify stuck on that song, again.

Shall I ask my colleagues currently
sending disguised goodbyes
on dating app chats, laughing
so they don't cry, or too busy friends?
What about those squeezing
a little more time as if the moment
their head turns they'll forget every freckle
or the woman sat next to me now
with only 6 weeks left to live?

DAY 135: NOTES

Yours were so smooth,
I barely noticed I was tapping my feet
until the evening's final song
when my own notes did not harmonise
and welcome your lips,
and with tomorrow's clear head,
I saw you miss a beat, make music,
not with me.

Your lips played in minor keys,
I stood in the clarity of my pitch,
as I watched yours slowly fading.

DAY 136: LULLABY

The best songs ever made
were written by parents.

There are so many ways
in which we love so much,

but we love one thing
so much

and are at a complete loss
for everything else.

Aren't we all children
scared to sleep alone?

Don't we all deserve
one last gentle memory

or kiss goodnight,
to be a lullaby?

DAY 137: A CAPPELLA

I used to believe a capella was the bee's knees,
but have you ever seen a capella groups fight

on the royal mile at the Ed Fringe Festival,
like something out of West Side Story?

Their fees are subsidised by universities,
so what are they trying so desperately to sell?

Who told these kids they're useless
unless they can pull a crowd?

THEME: EMOTIONS

The best and most beautiful things in the world cannot be seen or even touched. They must be felt with the heart.

Helen Keller

DAY 138: CALM

The tree that sways by the window,
watching me lay still through the glass,

The photographs in the living room,
watching my mind melt into the body,

The soft amber glow of the day closing,
watching me amble towards home.

DAY 139: ANGER

So much energy is spent on how angry to be,
if it is too much, too little, or whose fault it is,
that we never fully arrive where anger lives,
never open the door to air out and scream
until we've had enough and move out.

DAY 140: PRIDE

I too have pride in writing about this,
pride not writing about it, too much pride
to write about you, not enough pride
to write about me, too much pride to delete this,
and write what I so badly need you to know –
too proud to admit I missed the boat
    or overstepped.

DAY 141: DEPRESSION

She scratches at her own chest with an arrow,
making everyone accomplice to her slow death.
She wonders why people do not rush to save her,
do they not love her? She says.

The crowd shouts *pull it out or finish the job*,
and she decides they do not love her yet,
so she draws the bowstring even further back
but her fingers slip, and then –

DAY 142: THRILL

A cold shower,
standing on the edge of a cliff,
almost falling,
hearing a friend laugh their real laugh,
snorts and all.

DAY 143: JEALOUSY

I broke my own heart
and cracked grief in two –
I knew, I knew.

I'd chosen the losing
and the loss.

DAY 144: COMPASSION

You keep telling me
I deserve better.

But what if better
deserves you?

THEME: RAW MATERIALS

When you get close to the raw materials and taste them at the moment they let go of the soil, you learn to respect them.

Rene Redzepi

DAY 145: SILVER

We found silver to dig,
yet no triumph to remember.

DAY 146: SAND

2023, Jellyfish commit mass suicide on Porthcurno Beach.

I always loved watching Jellyfish saunter across
the sun-dappled waves, silvery and tinged with pink.

Today they're colourless and the ocean isn't speaking.

Onlookers point from the shore, they wave and scream,
thinking I'm drowning in the sea, but don't they know

the sea is drowning in me?

They can't see the little lifeless forms knocking into me,
their last attempt at making an impact.

I wash up on the beach like the jellyfish,
unable to sting and in pieces.

DAY 147: SOIL

A rain-soaked pinecone feasting on Mycelium,
its ringworm skin revealing a map
to my ancestral land.

Climbing an Oak to see what these giants behold,
secrets I can't possibly know from the ground,
being met with stoicism.

The wind refusing to spill, climbing down at dusk,
almost giving up, the soil opening up,
rooting me.

An ancient song: *you were born
with bark in your blood, soft moss,
deep path, sludge of mud.*

DAY 148: COTTON

Do you know where the ballots began?
With her hands, harvesting soft white clouds,

pulverising potential, stretching dreams
into a crisp blank page,

a room in which to decorate her future,
inking walls with brave notions

of who she was born to be,
who she was always becoming.

It was she who planted thee –
with soft hands and wild patience.

That's why when a woman writes,
it feels as though she's returned

from a long, long walk – her journey
started in the cotton fields,

and she's been walking towards
the page ever since.

DAY 149: GAS

One keeps us alive,
the other kills all life.
The details are in the process,
so why are we so obsessed
with the outcome?

DAY 150: LEATHER

Haría cualquier cosa por escuchar el *clink* familiar
de tu cinturón deslizándose por mi piso una vez más.

I didn't think it was an option, you said,
but we'd rolled too far over the conversation

to steer the truck back in that direction
even though it sounded like that's what you wanted.

I was so scared of watching you reverse over
your own boundaries that I hung up the phone.

I swear I heard that familiar *clink* as the line went dead.

DAY 151: SALT

My mum asks me why I look so sad,
and then leaves the room without waiting for an answer.

I almost tell her, but that song came on the radio,
the one that reminds me of us, of that time you left lunch

texting me as you sprang across the square.
It read: I miss you already.

I was going to tell her *you couldn't possibly*
but that you knew how special it would make me feel

as if our love was a river flowing between two banks
forever missing and meeting.

So your name fell into my coffee and drowned
like the dregs of a biscuit at the bottom of my cup

as my mum, unknowingly opening a box of moths,
left before the answer arrived, just like you

and who am I to pretend like this is the first
or the last time?

THEME: ANATOMY

Anatomy is to physiology as geography is to history; it describes the theatre of events.

Jean François Fernel

DAY 152: LUNG

I'd like to see your lungs up close,
hold them as gently as a fish in a hand
whilst they rise and fall to ask:

is this where breath is born?

If I listen closer than anyone has before,
would they tell me why they started,
would they tell me why they stopped?

DAY 153: MUSCLE

Count down from ten,
and allow each tight muscle,
a grand opening.
Sigh it out on seven
in one long unfurling.
The diaphragm will absorb
all that life is and can be,
at three, there's nothing you can't digest
or expel when two comes around.
So one it is, one thing left to do
   breathe.

DAY 154: TONGUE

Has
it
betrayed
you
too?

DAY 155: HEART

There is a reason why the word art
belongs in artery – how can anything that
carries blood from the heart and out
into the body not be the source
of all creative flow?

DAY 156: EAR

You are all I want to listen to,
so ask me every question on your tongue,
and I'll find every answer under it.

DAY 157: HIPS

She can feel the weight of you all,
even now.

DAY 158: SKULL

Think of all the people our skulls
have been within an inch of
and have never touched,

yet we think it's our hearts
that are lonely.

THEME: FABLES, MYTHS AND LEGENDS

*Myths and creeds are heroic struggles to comprehend
the truth in the world.*

Ansel Adams

DAY 159: SORCERESS

Any woman who has made others uncomfortable
simply by being alive has known the life of sorcery.

So tell me, how am I not witch enough,
and how much more witch can I be?

DAY 160: FAIRY GODMOTHER

I jumped on a plane as soon as she called,
dropped everything to be by her side,

arrived at her door with everything I had
and everything I didn't.

It's easy once you decide
to be the bridge between time,

which is nothing but a cloaked distance.

It is not a matter of *how long,*
or *what will this do for me,*

there are no excuses. The vacuum
that threatens to swallow us whole,

must be closed. We must appear before it,
hold out our hand, and do the right thing,

before the vacuum grows so large,
that nobody can see it.

DAY 161: DAMSEL

A small girl passes by the window,
disappearing, reappearing, clutching books.

She paces back and forth on the same floor.
I wonder if she is trying to find her way down,

but the door remains untouched.
She's looking up.

It's a beautiful tower hung with flowers,
though she does not seem to notice,

I doubt a dragon would disturb her,
even if it breathed fire.

She's intent on reaching places,
I could only hope to climb.

DAY 162: AXE

What is it about cutting off
parts of people, places and things
that we want to be rid of in our lives?

Haven't we learned by now?
Everything we cut, *multiplies.*

DAY 163: KING

I vowed never to follow a man into battle
but that was when I had no King

and all realms were full of Prince's
trying to be him.

Then I met a King who quiets armies in my heart,
quells unrest with an angel tongue and gentle touch,

alongside him, I am a Queen.

I vowed never to follow a man into anything,
but that was when I had no King.

DAY 164: VILLAIN

You swallowed my eyes
but now they see you from the inside,
you locked the truth away but one day
the pressure will set it free.

I watch you try to make your success louder
than your crimes, but I know what you did
so that you could climb.

When I stab you back in my dreams
I wake and realise, this must have been
the place you were in to do such
an unspeakable thing.

It dissolves any desire I have for revenge,
pity crawls over me, and I hope you heal,
even if you don't want to remember
the hand you held when you were in need.

I did not deserve what you did,
but revenge is never the key to freedom,
so I left to remain soft, that is how I know,
I'm not the villain you thought I was.

DAY 165: MERMAID

She softly hums her name,
the one that waits on the shore,
the song is caught in the ocean current,
the fish follow and I'm swept along
like a key being lifted to a lock.
The humming grows loud
and the slipstream swirls,
who am I now? Am I fish or girl?
I wash up on the shore,
kissing her feet
in a whole new world.

THEME: WONDERS OF THE WORLD

See the world. It's more fantastic than any dream.

Ray Bradbury

DAY 166: PYRAMID

Yesterday
I tried to build a life
top first and tumbled down.
I wanted to reach what was beyond
and not below, hunt before I gathered,
jump before I knew who or what would catch me.
Today, I know differently. I go back to the beginning
and build a stronger foundation word by word as an amateur.

DAY 167: GARDENS

We've planted so many with our abundant hearts,
when others would turn the ground and start again.
We nurtured such an abundant crop, our land was taken
and we were barred - no longer permitted to roam and enjoy
or tend to the fruits we sowed, because of those who wish
to erase the memories of seeds. Those creeping vines -
dead without a trellis to climb, you know who I mean.

DAY 168: TEMPLE

You are on the Poet's path,
both the pilgrimage and the temple,
the way as fragile as an orchid,
as essential as oxygen. Look at you –
descending towards Sacredness.
Where the rooms require real attention,
the walls do not call you lazy or late,
no furniture to carry, hoard, or hide in,
just the sound of your breath, your life,
with so much space.

DAY 169: STATUE

Catch that tear little eyelash, shield the rain,
make a wish little eyelash, share your pain,
shed all flesh and solidity so only eyelash remains,
have faith, little eyelash – the sun will rise again.

DAY 170: LIGHTHOUSE

All the women I know are lighthouses
on the cliffs of history, and you are one of them.

Look at your tall frame surveying the horizon,
seeing more than the naked eye ever could,

how you find the darkest recesses of the ocean,
locate the boat being tossed around like a mouse

flung about by a cat's claw.

Look how you shine a light on the boat,
trust it to find its bay, to make it home,

as it hurls itself against the current,
with nothing but your light to lead the way.

DAY 171: MAUSOLEUM

She thinks I don't notice how she tidies the house.
How can I not notice? When paper obituaries
smother the birthday cards, her cupboards –
a cemetery for other people's loose ends.
How can I not notice?

When she won't stop talking about the sorting,
the sorting that *must* be done. The trouble is,
she's so good at sorting, she's sorted herself away,
and I'm not sure in which pile of things she's buried.

DAY 172: COLOSSUS

I want to be huge – more gargantuan than *it*,
I want to open my mouth two whales wide

and swallow every bit of *it* out of this world,
out of you.

I don't want to chip away at stone
but break boulders with my bare hands.

From up here I am mighty strong,
as fearsome as the distance between us.

I shatter glass bottles with a heavy sigh,
obliterating *it* to dust.

From these heights, it's not lost on me
that you will never, *you will never*,

and I am not, *I am not.*

But even if I was, size has no relation
to strength or destruction.

Is this what it feels like to be you, God?

THEME: DEITIES

Human beings are co-partners with deity in the project of being.
This is the basis of all magic.

Terence McKenna

DAY 173: EOS, GODDESS OF THE DAWN

Most rendered her bare white heels
flashing under a nightgown too brief
to pay attention to their disappearance.
Only small gatherings arrived at her bed,
those that knew what the demons said
in the darkest nights, those that worshiped
Helios and Selene, meadow and cliff edge,
witnesses of rabbits becoming thrush bushes,
and birdsong – distant traffic.

DAY 174: HYPNOS, GOD OF SLEEP

I help everything die,
pickpocket half-baked habits,
churn memory into a memory of a memory,

feast on the day's breath
and dance on dreams until
they break apart like cotton candy.

You've no idea how lucky you are,
to mourn only morning,
noon and night

and not every lover you've kissed,
or lifetime you've lived. What use
is carrying it all into tomorrow?

DAY 175: DIONYSUS, GOD OF FESTIVITY

She is drunk and missing
and the world implodes while others dance.

I'm trying to find her with little alarm
but my heart knocks against my chest,

this place – a mass of arms and legs
and suddenly, there she is, ecstatic,

hands above her head, a wobbling Goddess
grabbing invisible fruit from the sky.

What is this? She says as I hand her
a glass of colourless liquid.

She rolls the glass to the floor like dice.
Odds it will smash! She squeals.

Her smile vanishes with the thud
of everything still in its place.

DAY 176: NEMESIS, GODDESS OF RETRIBUTION

A hall of mirrors as far as the eye can see.
You can't escape what you see,
and you do see it, don't you?

It's easy to see what is not, come closer,
get to know every inch, watch whatever is,
be whatever you deserve, a reckoning,

give it your full attention or else accept
no reflection, no point of reference,
just two eyes a nose, and a mouth,

hanging on a skull.

They call this the Hall of Mirrors.
Whatever you see could be Heaven,
or it could be Hell.

DAY 177: DEMETER, GODDESS OF HARVEST

There is a place I go to remember
what words cannot touch,

where rights and wrongs
will not reach,

where no sharp twigs
trip up feet.

It is the forest,
where I can tell the trees

I've been loved,
just as much as I haven't been.

DAY 178: PSYCHE, GODDESS OF THE SOUL

This is the Year of the Goddess, did you know?
I took a man through to climax without touching him,
made his body dance with an unintelligible tongue,
using only the space between my skin and his,
and we discovered the answers to everything.

DAY 179: MOIRAI, THE DEITIES OF DESTINY

The mother in you, the mother in me
and the mother in her, spun our hair
in the wheel, we are the homecoming,
we are the way back to our roots.

THEME: AUTUMN

No spring nor summer beauty hath such grace as I have seen
in one autumnal face.

John Donne

DAY 180: CRACKLING

The crackling fire, a crisp leaf,
the crunch of snow, the snap of a twig.
In Spring we'll sing of mending
but now is the time to rip.

DAY 181: BRISK

I've let the dead things fall,
and I am not one of those things.

DAY 182: DEW

When leaves wipe away,
the tears of Angels.

DAY 183: CHESTNUT

Come get your sweets
for the cold and lonely soul,
the insides look like little brains.

DAY 184: PUMPKIN

Mum and I turned stuffed peppers into Pumpkins,
sliced bananas in half, and dipped them in white chocolate
to make ghosts. We turned sausage rolls into mummies,
and biscuits and ice cream cones into witch's hats.
Hocus pocussing, hubbly bubbling, alchemising life
into a game with more joy than was possible that morning.

DAY 185: SAP

I've seen people
stick a tap in a tree
and swallow its insides,
they never once asked
if they could drink.

DAY 186: FORAGE

What have you found out here,
in the wild?

Makeup, plasters, tupperware, I see.
Odd socks, the odd memory encouraged
by song or scent. Cases: suit, brief, court.

Ah! *A wild strawberry fruit,*
and a lifelong friend or two,
that's more like it!

THEME: COSMOS

If you wish to make an apple pie from scratch,
you must first invent the universe.

Carl Sagan

DAY 187: ASTEROID

There is an Oscar Wilde quote that says:

When you are upset with not getting what you want,
just think about all of the things you didn't get
that you didn't want.

Let's spend today honouring missed-potential,
those life-shattering near misses that pass us
like an asteroid stroking the earth with its shadow.

DAY 188: STAR

If you're looking for a path,
choose a star, name her Teacher,
and study her across time and space.

DAY 189: LIGHT-YEAR

The me that sees the man
on this motorbike move, is the light
entering my eye, measuring the distance
between us.

How far are you from where you want to be?

DAY 190: BLACK HOLE

I want to know as little about black holes
as I can because black holes make the chasm of grief
tangible.

What's worse than emptiness?

We've almost begun to accept that life exists
outside of our control, but what about death

being out of control?

DAY 191: TIME-TRAVEL

If you want to know your way out of here,
there is an atlas of stars above your head,
echoes and imprints, wishes, and deaths.

As you search the sky, shouting names,
pointing to different parts of the same thing
- remember you're looking at time spent.

If you want to return to that last kiss,
watch the sunset. You have eight minutes
to realise what makes you ache,

and rise out of bed for, then like a star,
return to yourself and *implode.*

DAY 192: SPACESHIP

No spaceship came to save me,
I never once stopped to think
I was exactly where I was meant to be,
an alien in a strange land seeing things
deliberately *differently*.

DAY 193: UNIVERSE

Stars feel the pressure too,
the weight of the universe
presses down upon them
and are they impervious?

No darling - they explode.
So shatter gloriously.

THEME: ELEMENTS

Of the four elements, water is the second in weight and the second in respect of mobility. It is never at rest until it unites with the sea.

Leonardo da Vinci

DAY 194: EARTH

I have so much beautiful time
to wander and to roam,
if I measure not by minutes
burning quicker than I'd hoped.

I have so much beautiful time
being of the Earth,
life is a languid rhyme, our soft
womb and sombre hearse.

Being of the Earth,
and more than Earth I walk until
time is not a measurement,
time is what I will.

DAY 195: WATER

Tell her your dreams,
she has memory.
Share your fears,
she heals wounds.
Show her your failures,
she washes them,
with salt and spray.

DAY 196: FIRE

They burn more easily,
things that have known fire.

DAY 197: ICE

I can feel the crack of water
breaking against my teeth, me,
who is also made of water,
and the warming sun and the boats
and the humans who can't stop speeding
into unchartered waters and I think,
as I swallow the outcome, the ice caps
are melting in my mouth. Ice is alchemy.
How do I hide my own body, away, frozen,
for future generations to drink from
when there is nothing left to melt?

DAY 198: TIME

Connection doesn't know of calendars or clocks,
a soul is not a brain or a measuring jug,
a soul can't make an appointment,
can't be turned off or put on snooze,
it is a force fortified by contrast.

So if you want to fight and lose,
deny your soul what it loves
and blame it on time or distance.

DAY 199: THUNDER

Thunder threatens to alter all well-made plans,
like a spontaneous visit from the in-laws,
or the student throwing chairs around the classroom.
Someone is always secretly egging them on.

Go on! Make a raucous, shock us out of our lives,
scream and we'll scream too, so no one will know
we feel it, so no one knows we want to shake the world
out of ourselves and ourselves out of the world.

DAY 200: LIGHT

I've not heard from you in a while
and I know what that means.

I'm calling to you
from the corner of your room

where the lamp is,
I'm trying to turn it on.

I'll try the candle,
can you see it flickering?

Each dance of the flame
is a whisper saying

everything is going
to be okay.

THEME: FLOWERS

To plant a garden is to believe in tomorrow.

Audrey Hepburn

DAY 201: FORGET-ME-NOT

She wanted us to plant the seeds
after her funeral, but they're still in the packet.

I'm too scared to watch her die twice,
the last one would be my fault,

some mere oversight - too much water,
not enough sun.

I keep the seeds on the dresser
and she whispers,

forget-me-not, forget-me-not,
over and over like a parrot.

So I empty the seed packet
down my throat.

DAY 202: CHERRY BLOSSOM

It is winter in Andalucia
and I've never seen a Cherry Blossom
bear fruit. In the UK we name things

because we like to be ironic, but here,
cherry blossoms blossom cherries.
This is how I imagine it feels

to experience childhood without
the shattered remnants of a promise
from a parent broken inside of you.

DAY 203: ORCHID

I once saved an Orchid from the trash,
my ex had taken it upon himself to play God.

When he'd first given the plant to me,
the petals were dyed a garish blue and showed off.

When it hadn't flowered for a while,
and without asking me, he threw it away.

He never did see the beauty
in deflowered things.

DAY 204: LOTUS

As I watch you fold and unfold again,
a light touches your right shoulder,
you take a deep breath and something leaves.

Grace is the arrangement of your face
and you've never been so patulous,
so timeless and divine.

As I watch you fold and unfold again,
I wish to hold you and carry you
to lighter days.

Instead, I watch you churn the stream of grief
like a mill turning that which can't be dammed
out of your body, and into the light.

DAY 205: LILLY

I don't want to be kissed.
I want to scream so loud
the fates rush a friend
back from the grave.
I want the little girl in class
not to hide her book
and parade around
an ill-fitting bra.

I want to be the first ancestor.
I want to gather dead bodies
dropping on the scorched earth
and give birth to their future.
I want to be the girl
before she meets grief.
Which means somewhere,
I'm twelve years old,
crying out to be kissed.

DAY 206: DANDELION

We try to remember some people to be kind,
but in truth, many things are carried away on the wind
and never thought of again. Memories are pulled from minds
like weeds and scattered, whilst someone else can't look away,
trying to memorise the route as if that could stop the wind
from taking away what isn't theirs.

THEME: JOURNEY

We don't travel to move around, we travel in order to be moved.

Pico Iyer

DAY 207: DESTINATION

Where next?
  Or
Where now?

DAY 208: TRANSIT

Ode to the Long Bus Journey

I'm finally telling you after all this time,
that my life hangs between getting on that bus
and taking it as far as it will go

and all of the stuff I busy myself with to try and stay,
to try and quieten the perpetual desire to be in transit,
leaving and never arriving –

DAY 209: WANDER

When have you ever picked joy
and felt less joy? When have you ever
run out of love by using too much?
When has wonder ever caused
disillusion? When did wandering
ever make you too busy?

DAY 210: SOLITUDE

The voice has gone astray,
and I'm writing with my mind,
trying to finish this well ahead of time.
You want me to be here,
and they want me to be there,
but I must write in solitude,
to grow what I must share.

DAY 211: MAP

Do you need to know
where you will end up?

DAY 212: LOST

I try to find my way back and every time,
I know no one and no one knows me.
After a while, it becomes harder to return,
back becomes a circle to where I am,
and where I am going, and I wonder
why I set out in search of meaning.

DAY 213: ARRIVE

Deja Vu

In a forest in Switzerland I lay on my back
on the floor in the van, crossing my leg over
in a yoga pose, staring up at the wooden ceiling.
  Oh. I've been here before.

My body has caught up with the future.

Like a cog it's clicked with all the choices ever made
and not made and so made either way, I am *in place*.
We are here. Both of us, the me that was already there,
and the me that is newly arriving.

THEME: TAROT

Tarot and dreams are two dialects in the language of the soul.

Philippe St Genoux

DAY 214: THE WHEEL OF FORTUNE

Prosper in the dim dark alleyways of your life,
the narrow corridor telling you where you can go,
parallel walls with space for others to try and escape.

Touch the bricks to see what lies feel like,
before they crumble into dust, this is another mirage,
spin the wheel and wait, or move the wheel and decide.

DAY 215: THE CHARIOT

This is what it feels like to move
beyond your old schedules and plans:
Leaning too far back on a swing,
being driven down a hilly road,
being launched into space.

DAY 216: THE FOOL

My parents played The Fool so fools could not play them,
showing me how to shake laughter from my body
like water off a duck's back.

I was never good at pretending,
I was only ever meant for what I was,
a porous sack of teardrops that swelled when squeezed.

DAY 217: THE LOVERS

Before you went to Canada I saw the number 2222022
as the number of your train. No other train had a number
anything like that one. I went home and Google said things like
union, twin-flame, you're life is going to change,
new beginnings, love.

You don't believe in signs like me,
but even you couldn't deny what came next.

DAY 218: THE MAGICIAN

Open, pen your dreams, open dreams penned in, peel off skin around words that lack substance, bankrupt actions, banquets of banked ideas and banal thoughts banned from the busy bazaar in that bunk bed in your head. Bank on that, deposit ink and pen, dip your finger in blood, draw all outcomes you can think of, then scrawl over your own spells, because you can, you, the magician, who wields words into worlds, into whatever space spools salaciously from sockets seldom seen, open, *oh* pen your dreams.

DAY 219: THE DEVIL

The devil is not so bad,
always up for a pint or a laugh,
but never around to face the trouble,
when you stagger home at 5 am,
reeking of mistakes.

DAY 220: THE HERMIT

A woman must have money and a room of her own if she is to write fiction.
Virginia Woolf, A Room of One's Own

A woman must have a desk large enough to leverage the cosmic powerhouse of her magic if she is to write.

A woman must sit at a south-facing window in which to see her potential fly if she is to write.

A woman must have a canine companion to give limitation to structure and space for her to love something that isn't writing if she is to write.

A woman must have her own apartment with rooms spacious enough to dance in and remember life is for living if she is to write.

A woman must fiercely guard her solitude if she is to write.

A woman must have a friend who writes, so she can be seen without having to stop writing if she is to write.

A woman must have a lover or companion who doesn't write and who can't possibly understand but loves her enough to make tea, coffee, lunch, and dinner, during the writing, jokes during the editing, wipe her tears during re-drafting, and hold her through the night after submission if she is to write.

A woman must have silence from all the ghosts who tried to kill her because they could not contain her if she is to write.

A woman must get past the point where not writing feels like dying if she is to write.

A woman must know that if all that seems impossible, a woman can write if she is to write.

A woman must have the audacity to write if she is to write.

.

THEME: CREATURES

Imagination will often carry us to worlds that never were.
But without it, we go nowhere.

Carl Sagan

DAY 221: WEREWOLF

Do you not see us? Neck craning to the moon,
fur growing wilder with each phase,
a thirst for the blood of all who wronged us,
wide eyes, indifferent, yellow in the light,
and a howl that curls the edge of everything?

DAY 222: KRAKEN

She Will Intensify the Way the Ocean Does
After Wild Embers by Nikita Gill

I'm the northerly wind on a ship's sail,
guiding wayfarers home from the shore,

but I want to be She who swallows shackles
of saltwater until harbours are harbours no more.

She who drowns trespassers, bashes their bones
then spits them out in the direction

of whatever they've decided they own,
(which is nothing and nowhere and not me).

Only fully looked upon at the last,
she performs a furious baptism,

as black and green tentacles
conduct an orchestra of waterlogged screams,

as She sings all she is, *Kraken, Kraken!*

DAY 223: CYCLOPS

I have a lazy eye which people cared less about
when I was a child. I was gifted an eye patch
and looked too much like a Pirate to be bullied.

I became the lead role in the playground.
One day they replaced the eye patch with glasses,
ugly flowery things. *Pirates don't wear glasses,* I said.

I learned then that glasses never fix,
take them away, and what do you see?

DAY 224: SIREN

The child does not cry,
the dog does not bark,
the father does not shout,
and the sirens do not ring.

The child shouts
while the father barks,
as the dog rings
and the sirens cry.

Life is not a list or a script,
but a flower or fist,
ripples of water around
a skimmed stone.

Life is dough
folding in on itself.

DAY 225: DRAGON

I was riding a dragon and flying it
around the Isles in Scotland
with a guy I had a crush on at uni.
I can't remember if I screwed him,
or killed him. Probably both.
He has a baby now, with a girl
who was so young, a girl
I would have wished to be before
I woke up from that dream.

DAY 226: YETI

I want a pet yeti
to cuddle when I'm blue,
to scare away all evil things,
and make me laugh a little too.
They say the Yeti isn't real,
but sometimes I do find,
the Yeti is alive in all of us,
abominably silly,
and abominably kind.

DAY 227: PHOENIX

Every feather is the face
of those who have given
fire to my rise.

THEME: HERBS AND SPICES

When our hands have touched spices, they give fragrance to all they handle.

John Vianney

DAY 228: CINNAMON

If I were a spice I'd claim Cinnamon,
and dance within tea, pie and buns.

DAY 229: MINT

As I retired with a belly full of day
and your song came on, the one you played
as a ghost at your funeral as if music made you eternal,
I realised I've been holding my breath since you died.

The tears came, dislodging a piece of my tongue
and the silence left like a friend who realised
they'd outstayed their welcome.

It could have been the mint-scented shampoo
that cleared my airways or maybe it was you,
reminding me that I was still breathing,
and not to stop.

DAY 230: SAFFRON

Take me to your orange smoke
 and purple caves.

DAY 231: SAGE

Do you notice that when you look at something,
I mean, really pay attention, other people look too?

Try it now on the tube or in class, use your power
of attention. You see it, don't you?

Bearing witness is not a waste of time.
Choose your gaze, and the gaze of others will follow.

So if you want to stop a war, stare into the eyes of joy,
run at her as if you are running into a lover's arms,
show us where to look, and help us to see her.

DAY 232: ROSEMARY

I can't wait to build my own garden, he says,
as we stroll just shy of the mist-covered peaks,
dew in our hair, fingers lightly brushing sage bushes,
and sprigs of wild rosemary.

We feast on wild fruit from a strawberry tree,
(because the app said it was okay) and leave the mushrooms
(because the app couldn't decide).

I pick up a pinecone and he tells me,
this is where pine nuts come from. Can you believe
I'd never made the connection? The pinecones I know of,
sit in a basket in the corner of the living room and do nothing
but collect dust. I decide to keep it for the new garden.

We pass a fruiting olive tree. *We'll come back for those olives,
and bring them home*, we tell each other, our pace slowing
as we approach a bend in the road towards the city.
My stomach tenses and the pinecone speaks,
leave me here, please.

DAY 233: TURMERIC

Make tea, make anything to keep these hands busy.
Make eggs, and beat them because they're already dead.
Make a blanket of Tumeric to cover the crime.
Make tea, make anything, make a noise like a laugh.
Make time to go outside and see the sky look like beaten eggs
swimming under a blanket of Tumeric.

Realise there is no beating the sky, only ourselves.
It's no use, there's not enough left in the bowl. So.
Make Orange Rooibos with a splodge of honey.
Make anything to keep these hands busy.

DAY 234: BASIL

A potted plant is not love,
but we'll try anyway,
pull leaves where we can
to give blandness flavour.

THEME: WINTER

It is the life of the crystal, the architect of the flake, the fire of the frost, the soul of the sunbeam. This crisp winter air is full of it.

John Burroughs

DAY 235: FROST

Winter freezes reason
and keeps tree corpse's cold,
for Spring to softly heal them
so Summer can be bold, she paints
by number each eager branch,
that Autumn soon drapes gold,
for the wind to sneeze away with love,
the weight of all they hold.

DAY 236: CHRISTMAS TREE

Oh
little tree
that fills us with joy,
your spiky hair does not have
to brush the ceiling to make hearts sing.
Hanging with memories from a cherished past,
we love you on the wonk and bare in places.
We love you fake and unkempt
and wonder at our
Christmas miracle.

DAY 237: ELF

The thing I love about Christmas
is the two café owners at Walton Station
and the way we pick up the same conversation
years between seeing each other.
I love the girl sitting across from me
on the train to Waterloo
who smiles at random thoughts in her head,
her memories waking up her face,
a moment only I see, a moment only she feels.
I love the orange light peering
from the grey clouds over London,
the fact that I'm not rushing
and that my breakfast fits in my pocket,
that I'm dressed inadvertently like a Christmas Elf,
or Waldo from Where's Wally – that I look eccentric
in my red and green amongst the grey and black,
that I know joy within pain, that I am the kind of person
who notices, as if for the first time.

DAY 238: NATIVITY

It hurt like hell and there was blood everywhere.
There were so many greedy eyes in one room,
I wanted to poke them out, but the hay was too soft
and would've bent before it pierced.

The wise men told me I was *blessed.*
I want to make them pregnant with a story
that swells in their belly and gives them cankles.

How could they all look at me, nodding nobly
like I just magicked this up? Only Joseph,
his eyes turned up to the sky, only he knows.

Mealtimes have never been quieter,
but the plates aren't empty. We pray alone
or not at all these days, and the words stick
in our mouths like sawdust.

Joseph acts as if this happened to him,
which he thinks it has. They came for my womb
because I was ovulating and nothing else.

A hundred beautiful and glorious children
are being born every minute and this one

is the Son of God?

The group wasn't gathered neatly around the crib,
they were stepping over each other to get into frame,
like an awkward wedding photo, in the Midwife's way.

I say Midwife. I mean the Innkeeper's wife,
who can now add babies to the list of things she pulls,
a pint glass is about the same size.

She never made it into the story,
they would've had to make her a saint,
but Saint Candy didn't sound right.

No one mentioned that the donkey
started shitting so everyone had to leave
because of the smell.

I didn't notice. My darling baby boy
had the face of an angel, I was too busy
believing the story they wanted to tell.

DAY 239: GIFT

The world crowds around the gifted man,
but god is not the gifted man, god is the crowd
realising it created something more than itself.
God has shown up to listen to his own work.
The piano player shares not their gifts
with the world, but the world's gifts,
shows themselves to God,
and God to himself.

DAY 240: SOUP

You are Chicken Soup
in the bowl of Winter,
home-made and buttery,
salty and delicious, a flavour
that lingers on the tongue.

DAY 241: SCARF

Your gritty tongue wets the mouth
with the promise of a new day.

You've found us drifting far too long
aboard a duck feather ship,

dreaming under a sea of sheets
on this springy shore.

Your quivering body around my neck
becomes a black and honeyed fur scarf,

I inhale cheesy feet flavoured popcorn,
a scent only a dog parent could love.

You skip rainbow-shaped on your soft play of pillows,
and check that we're still watching.

There's no chance of us getting some skin on skin
- you dart in and snuggle your way into our hearts.

THEME: FAMILY

In every conceivable manner, the family is link to our past, bridge to our future.

Alex Haley

DAY 242: BROTHER

Chalk and cheese, gym and pizza,
alcohol and phones, knowledge and Jon Snow.
One pot, two plants, born in the same house,
one opened bright flowers, and the other grew roots
so deep into the Earth, they may never show.

DAY 243: GRANDDAD

My Grandad used to say *a shed is just a shed,*
perhaps a mispronunciation of *let's call a spade a spade.*

Writing lists of everything a shed could be,
I should have known then it was a Poet's life for me.

The world is a shed at the end of the Galaxy's garden,
storing us until the season is ready for our use.

A body is a shed, and a mind, and your heart.
Life is a shed, fear is a shed, love too.

A shed is just a shed, Granddad,
but it's also everything.

DAY 244: DAUGHTER

And he tries so very hard
to think of the right thing
to say to his unborn daughter,

how to protect her,
keep her from harm,
avoid danger.

He tries so very hard
to find the right thing
he can tell her to do,

so she will be safe,
so she can be safer,
learn how to be safe.

After ten minutes
of listening politely,
we always listen,

I whisper, *yes love*
but what will you say
to your sons?

Little hope is found
on his furrowed brow,
a future father

who tries *so very hard*,
but whose daughter
must try harder.

DAY 245: SISTER

West Molesey Cemetery

Kalopsia was my mum's recipe for life,
but all I saw was a stone statue of a chubby baby
wearing a hat of bird poo trying to resemble
a smiling cherub watching over my Sister Violet.
I watched topsoil being watered by mourners' tears,
juicy fat worms sleeping it off after the best
buffet of their lives, the imprint of a right boot
trampling every dead thing to find its other half,
(when we were sure they'd loved us most),
clever set-design constructing the fourth wall,
sickly plastic petals coughing into the wind
and an ill-tempered scuff of dirt, mine.
When I think you got off lightly. When I think
if you'd lived, we could've shielded each other,
I come here to remind myself that life
isn't about seeing things as more beautiful
than they are, it's knowing we are an entry
on a balancing sheet with no room
for error or discussion.

DAY 246: NAN

A sea of smoke swirling around the living room.
I crawl in, elbows risk carpet burn, inhale,
shout something about dinner being ready,
and crawl back out, she never takes
her eyes off the TV.

DAY 247: COUSIN

Did you slip past me when I'd finished work
and felt the bright sun embrace me? Or when a friend texted,
telling me she loved me, without saying why?

It could have been in the restaurant when I swapped
the empty candle holder for a lit flame,
which snuffed out as soon as laughter touched it,

or why my skin tingled as we pondered poetry and travel,
perused the menu like it was an Atlas and raised a toast:
To Opportunity.

Was it half a second behind the beep of my oyster card?
Mid-step, three-quarters from the way home or the C minor
twang of my keys kissing the ring on my index finger?

When my torso hit forty-five degrees from ceiling to pillow?
Hello? I have to be sure that I wasn't sleeping on the job,
that you weren't stuck behind my last thought of the day,

I need to know if I jolted awake that same night because
my body felt the clock strike *loss* or if it really was my dog
that led me outside because I have a feeling it was you

blinking back at me as I searched the stars and smiled,
thankful to be alive.

DAY 248: AUNTIE

There is a picture of her in dungarees,
standing in front of Hampton Court Bridge,
staring straight into the soul of the camera,
relaxed yet ready, for what? No idea.

She was in the Army, and I tell everyone,
as if her strength becomes my own,
or maybe I copy the way Mum does it.

Working in Intelligence, she kept many secrets,
her frame elegant, and her style effortless,
darkness lingering behind her eyes,
enemy present and undetected.

THEME: WILDLIFE

The wildlife and its habitat cannot speak, so we must and we will.

Theodore Roosevelt

DAY 249: ROBIN

A fat lone Robin,
no care for its loneliness,
sings in the snowdrift.

DAY 250: FOX

I blend into the city like this skulking fox,
struck by the scent, following its nose
to where lives lollop and drag
through the trash.

In the ancient Capital of Europe,
I can't stop staring at the dumpsters
that can't catch what's thrown out
quicker than it's collected.

My neighbour beats his dog,
there is no desk to write or
place to talk with the night sky,
I used to be a bird,
now I'm half fox,
half trash.

DAY 251: HEDGEHOG

The nation's sweetheart,
celebrity cutie on Nature's TV
and small ball of stick art.

DAY 252: ELEPHANT

Two truths and a lie:

There is an almond tree growing in the park
near my house and I am thrilled you are gone,
no mark of grief, your eyes do not haunt me.

I met someone else while I was busy
trying to love an almond tree, we met in a bar
called *El Poema*.

In the darkness of night with eyes soft focus,
it could be him lying there.

DAY 253: PYTHON

I am no longer willing to compromise,
an act born from the back of a forked tongue
like making two people walk in time
while one is pulled and the other pushed,
tied to the same line. So do not do that for me
and I shall not do that for you, cut us both free,
and we shall love each other till the end of our lives
or not but at least our lives are ours to move,
our bones harbouring a far gone memory, any time
we are about to accept less so as not to offend.

DAY 254: OWL

My eyes are searchlights searching the void.
Are you here because you're searching twit-twoo?

Wide-eyed and open-mouthed, spinning heads
360 degrees to catch any sign of it flying past.

DAY 255: HYENA

They laugh because
  we think.

THEME: NATURAL DISASTERS

*In all natural disasters through time, man needs to attach meaning to tragedy,
no matter how random and inexplicable the event is.*

Nathaniel Philbrick

DAY 256: ERUPTION

I don't want to write this poem,
I avoid typing anything
that may hold me to account
because as much as I want to be fluid –
I am not. I do not shape-shift,
my shape is set for today
like my arms now buried
in someone else's black top
(it barely dares to touch my skin),
legs squashed into dark blue jeans,
feet reclining on boots bought in Sorrento
(because I can't bear to feel morose
on the outside too), the Primark ring
that makes my finger green, but can't throw
because the past holds weight.
I don't want to carry this poem on,
I'm a volcano about to erupt,
and I don't want to be like the scribes,
watching the disaster from afar
so we can build museums for inaccuracy
and say that nothing could be done.
I don't want to know in which formation
my face will solidify, I want to be my shadow,
featureless, so I don't have to admit,

I can't bear you looking at me like that,
I can't bear me looking at me like that.
My face flushes and something boils.
I run from the room, put my head in the freezer
and lay dormant for the next few years.

DAY 257: LANDSLIDE

Intense, he mouths to me as his brother's voice
ricochets down the banister, bouncing word bombs
down the hallway.

He tries to escape to the shops as his siblings shout
at one another from alternate universes, uncaring
if they receive a reply before they begin the next thread.

The familiarity makes my knees weak,
it swims in the coffee handed to me at breakfast,
soaks in the bacon grease and grumpiness,

oozes from a brother deflecting orders via a screen,
a tween trying to find their identity in the cutlery draw,
a single mum touching everything in the kitchen all at once,

dogs weaving between feet, chattering knives and forks.
The ruckus settles between their shared passion for bagels.

The mum says, *do you like this?* I want to say,
I can't distinguish the egg between the bacon and the cheese
between the bagels but instead, I say *I want a family.*

This happens when you were minus before birth,

always playing catch up, seeing more than you need to,
and never being as close as you'd like to be.

Remember when boys told us we don't have to be wives?
We should want to be independent, it's sexy now,
to be fiercely unbothered about marriage, about anything.

Here is something *intense*: I want to vow, I want to mum,
to hear my sons kicking stones on the drive, slamming doors
and shaking the house, jumping the last two steps on the stairs,
killing parts of the earth they can't understand
within five seconds, and then I'll do what I do best,
soften the murderer out of them

until they stop trampling flowers
and start planting them.

DAY 258: TSUNAMI

Tomorrow the shelves will not be stacked,
stackers will be shelved to make way
for pixels – now personal shoppers.
Loo roll will roll on out of town
because trees will no longer stand for us.
AI will shoot algorithms at abandoned cars
in an attempt to get the ozone layer back,
who filed for divorce when we voted
for the first Green MP who celebrated
by driving down a street in Brighton,
in a pink Cadillac, throwing money
to gardeners who spent it all on weed killer.

DAY 259: HURRICANE

I was born into the world in a hurricane storm,
no one knew when it would end, but we did know
how to brace our bodies for impact.

There was some calm, in the eye,
whispered giggles under a tablecloth,
untouchable gods amongst pillars of feet.

Those places were temples of respite,
but we did not know those words,
we just felt left alone, unbothered, forgotten.

The hurricane raged for years, and quite suddenly,
was gone. Perhaps I outran it or swallowed it
and took its voice. Or was I the calm, the eye?

Always in the midst, never separate,
never will be, never done,
and with no warning,
I'll be gone.

DAY 260: EARTHQUAKE

It happens as we go about our work and leisure,
the unexplainable wave rippling in the coffee foam,
the almost invisible rattle of a cup on a china plate.

Tectonic plates have split underneath somebody's feet,
subsiding the ground, and making a hole big enough
to swallow someone they know.

If that's too much to think about now, let's be glad
that poetry is just poetry and not an earthquake,
simply an aftershock acknowledging itself,

a weather reporter informing the world
that someone is astride two flanks of Earth, splitting.

DAY 261: FLOOD

I can't stop writing about family.
It's like taking in too much sea water
unable to gasp for air when you need it,
choking it out, blind panic while you try
to stay afloat. I didn't expect this.
No one expects a flood when it comes,
that's why it's called a flood and not a
swimming pool, something contained,
that doesn't move as we get ready
to jump in.

Perhaps this is why I love swimming,
and find the sea unsettling.

DAY 262: BLIZZARD

Revealing a glimpse of what was to be,
amongst the silence in the snow drift,
absorbing all knowledge that things
were going to work out, a blizzard

blew us into the path of James Cordon.
He twisted around in alarm as Mum and I
burst through the hospital doors during
rehearsals for a comedy TV show.

Trains weren't running and the snow was deep,
but we'd taken too many buses and dragged
our suitcases too far through the snow,
two little robins trying to find a bough.

It was the first time I'd seen my Dad cry,
maybe he realised after all this time,
that we weren't *useless*, maybe
he always knew and couldn't bear

our innocence, our eagerness to please,
two little robins fluttering around,
chests red and plump, still warm.

THEME: LANGUAGE

For last year's words belong to last year's language
And next year's words await another voice.

T.S. Eliot

DAY 263: PUNCTUATION

I've never been good at economics.
When trying to behave my hand
gets stuck in a funk

lines akimbo in a frizz of angles

words
ker
plunk
like
marbles

as I shoot black sticks that curve
like a plane taking off a runway.

When trying to behave
my fingers are a faulty train

and it takes ten minutes to get going
before the window replaces the page.

At the end of the line, the tannoy
makes an announcement:

Something has been hit. I jump out
and see what the fuss is about.

Inspiration lay paralysed
between parallel tracks.

DAY 264: ACCENT

In the Spanish language,
the funny little 'n' with a squiggly hat
or 'eñe', pronounced like the *Gno* in Gnocci,
is the difference between:

Happy New Year (Feliz Año Nuevo)
and
Happy New Anus (Feliz Ano Nuevo)
and
I have thirty-three years (Tengo treinta y tres años)
and
I have thirty-three anuses (Tengo treinta y tres anos)

and yes I found out the hard way
to save you some trouble.

DAY 265: BRACKETS

The last goodbye tries not to be the end,
or what it is – a rift in time. It tries not to wake
the house, tries to live in brackets (don't wait up),
and loves to dress up in costume, its favourite,
the echo: *see you, see you, see you, see you* –

DAY 266: EMPHASIS

History suggests
that after lovemaking,
you must sweetly say *Uh–huh*
with emphasis on both syllables
so it won't sound like *ugh.*

Experience suggests
that after lovemaking,
you must sweetly say *Dar-ling,*
with emphasis on both syllables
so he knows you're not done speaking –

you reminded me of a Rhinoceros
climbing up a muddy bank.

DAY 267: SENTENCE

Dear Author,

I've found out your secret. Is that why it never ends,
why I will never be with you in your world?
I was made for another, seeking the Golden Jumper,
in a story - not of your genre.

I toppled through loose stitching that binds the book,
hooked onto the curve of a g, (swung nose-first into brackets)
stood naked in-between double spaces, rolled my full stop
like Sisyphus as penance for long sentences, and survived,

for what?

DAY 268: HYPHEN

The hyphen is a punctuation mark used to join words
and to separate syllables of a single word. A hyphen (-)
joins two words to have one meaning.

Can-some-one-put-me-in-touch-with-the per-son
who-can-help-me-be-come-the-next-best-mo-ther-
fun-kin-ev-er-y-thing-where-I-ev-en-have-to-hy-phen-
ate-how-much-I'm-worth-be-cause-it's-too-much-to-say-
in-one-sen-tence.

DAY 269: SPELLING

Friends and readers from the USA,
forgive me if you recognise awful spelling,
this book is a labour of love and if you knew,
that writing is my favourite thing, you may not know
I grew up in the theatre and learnt my trade by doing.
There's no need to analyse poems to know
what makes them great, expression is my colour
and there's no need for hateful judgement.
Although these spelling errors may make this poem grey,
a poem is a poem and should be honoured just the same.

DAY 270: GRAMMAR

I couldn't go back home, the street was cordoned off
due to *"men" working,* so I rushed to a public loo but it said
Toilet ONLY for disabled elderly pregnant children.
I ran to the field to do it in the bushes but the sign read,
Hunters please use caution when hunting pedestrians
using walk trails – so I gave that a wide birth
and hid behind a car but as I was halfway through
a policeman came and gave me money. I looked
at a note on the car which said that anyone caught
violating the vehicle, would be found fifty pounds.
So I went to Sport's Bar and waited till the work was done,
great guy, Sport.

THEME: ENDINGS

Great is the art of beginning, but greater is the art of ending.

Henry Wadsworth Longfellow

DAY 275: UNRAVEL

January
    I make friends with the stars
    and magic is born inside me.

February
    I tell you I want to kiss you
    and the world doesn't implode.

March
    I plant seeds that spring up like Daisies,
    and dance under Orange Blossom.

April
    I find my soulmate and we write
    our initiation into being.

May
    We open locked doors
    and we do not run away.

June
    I get sick and he has to leave
    and nothing is the same again.

July
   London, I remember why I left,
   my birthday slips by barely noticed.

August
   Suprise festival work gifts two friends,
   living in a field heals a five-year illness.

September
   We are giants astride the sea,
   making dreams with angels.

October
   A new city brings darkness,
   a new job brings sickness.

November
   A time for falling,
   tiny embers try to light me.

December
   I return home and unravel,
   the foam mattress remembers.

DAY 276: TEARS

I have acquired two stray cats,
they're trapped in the neighbour's empty flat.

I fling food over the fence when they meow,
which sounds like *help, help.*

I'm jealous of their ability to ask
and tears come in small bursts,

like a clapped-out car, trying to start,
or the clearing of the throat.

If I keep flinging food in their direction,
if I meow, someone will hear my plea,
and fling a lifeline back.

DAY 277: DEBT

I have nightmares about being a bad investment.
I'm tired of being in debt, I'll never pay it all back.
I'm losing lives faster than I'm creating them,
The Buddhist Monk, The Holistic Witch, The President,
The Priestess, The Sage Poet, The Animal Whisperer,
The Relationship Coach, The Guru, The Mother.
They're not convinced I'm worth the risk
and they're all asking for their money back.

DAY 278: ARREST

I've never been in Prison,
but I have been inside,

cling film across the front door,
water turned off at the throat.

DAY 279: FALLING

A kind of half-light, the click
of a switch between on and off,
it doesn't matter, anyway,

I could find a million metaphors
to describe what it feels like to return here
more times than we're willing to count.

Forget the scouring of yourself
for unique gifts or redeeming qualities,
use what you have, what you can.

Take from the world around you,
it's a bustling marketplace of busy fingers,
quick to share their wares between worlds

hoping they may catch the switch
on the way down.

DAY 280: FREEDOM

I imagine he goes down on one knee
at Lake Louise, and I tell him
he is the love of my life.
I should be the happiest girl in the world,
but I am a frozen lake
so I find a Spare Corner of the Earth,
a convent slash bathroom,
and close the door.

The ice sings before it breaks
and I swim alone in all their names,
and ugly cry. I snort and a laugh surprises me,
I know you are the least like them.
Why does that feel wrong?
Now I'm laughing in starts
like an engine trying to turn over
because they did not take my ability
to love and be loved and I think,
how will I ever be able to explain this?

The door opens and there he is,
face drenched with tears.
He picks me up off the floor
and whispers my name,

and the lake thaws
and for the first time in my life,
I'm glad there isn't a lock
on the bathroom door.

DAY 281: CRASH

My body has the power to pivot on its heel
yet I find myself missing the company of clouds.
I've never seen a cloud change direction,
what else can I watch that I do not own
and can't contain or move with mere thought
and then I remember I was a cloud once,
floating towards motherhood
before the formation broke.

DAY 282: INJURY

I knew it before I heard it,
and I felt it before I saw it.

A good mountain dog I'd say,
but dogs were never meant

to climb beds so high
that even I had to jump,

but she followed me to death.

When I heard her face
hit the cold marble floor,

I knew that look was coming,
trying to understand the pain

by looking into my eyes
with a tilted, shaking head

and mine, unable to answer.

DAY 283: BETRAYAL

When we have been betrayed, deeply and irretrievably,
we try to make a success out of our lives, to wield
injustice and turn it into triumph.

After betrayal, if we should like to use that word
after being pierced by it, (I think we'd like to remove
that word from the dictionary), real success,

is to go away for a long while and tell no one.

Here, we reunite with joy and gentleness,
introduce our shy selves to sensitive skin,
sing, *you hurt me and I can't hurt you back.*

We don't make a career out of it,
we spoon the black soil out of us,
small heap by small heap, until we're free
of everything we never agreed to carry.

Those people who harmed us
did not care for our fall,
why would they care for our rise?

They aren't thinking of us.

Let's take ourselves away,
put our arms around our hearts,
sit next to a warm fire and read.

The next day, we'll plant something.
Only the seed will know it has been planted.
That is true success to end all disquiet.

DAY 284: SEPARATE

The wind is fighting the trees,
nature does not recognise itself.

DAY 285: STOP

Everything stops, the birdsong,
his brain, as I hold him in my arms
unsure if he will breathe again.
I open the front door and find nothing,
no time, nor relief, no one to care.

That hour he left me, who knows where he went,
but on his return, my world moved again.

DAY 286: DIAGNOSIS

He does not want to carry the word
for the rest of his life and who am I to make him?

I watched him rearrange the words pouring
from the professional's mouth into a more
palatable pill.

What use is a word anyway?
We only touch its consequence.
And I will.

DAY 287: WANE

Everything is on the other side of build,
two moons rotating around the same star
playing kiss chase.

DAY 288: EXPIRY

I wondered when the time would come
for me to realise you never wanted to be a poem,
and there is something about his sigh,
how he turned up in my street calling my name
how he went to me, how loudly, that tells me
you and I are out of date.

DAY 289: WASTE

Dust has no impact
except to steal our attention
when it falls into the light,
playing charades with time
and our minds as we ask,
how is there this much dust?
Our bodies dancing side to side,
grasping fistfuls of the past.

DAY 290: GONE

The scream was palpable.
The dachshund thought his life had ended
as he fell over his own face under a huge paw.

They all laughed as he slowly limped
towards his owner, who was also laughing,
for the same reason Gorillas grin at the Zoo.

I could not speak the language,
but the man felt my fury and called after me,
waving the stick he used to keep the beast in line.

I walked away, impervious to the stick.
I can't promise I'll walk away next time.

DAY 291: BURN

He burns worry away
by leaning in when my body
screams to be outside of itself.
That is a fire to stoke,
to gather around
and where I go now,
in the minus of night
under fading stars,
to keep these cold bones
warm.

DAY 292: ASH

The ash of experience
can give light too.

DAY 293: BURY

I want to be eaten by the Earth,
why should I not give myself to her
of all places? I'm not meant to be
in a box on a shelf, I am the box, the shelf.
Bury me under a tree in Snowdonia.
Gather and read poetry, sing songs,
and share your fears. I'll listen
and kiss the breeze into your hair.

DAY 294: EULOGY

We imagine death a thousand times
before we release a poem out into the world,
so we know how to leave ourselves discoverable
in the afterlife, that is, the life after us,
that goes on, a life where our poems
are post-mortems, full of insight
that we never truly understood alive,
containing a truth that the living,
can't survive without.

DAY 295: BREAK

Broken Down Near Venice

All that is left are the crumbs of croissants
and the dregs of a shared orange juice.

When we return to the hotel room,
I head straight to the bathroom

without the energy to shut the door,
I sit on the toilet, hold my head in my hands,

and listen to the click of a photo being taken.

He is trying to find out what the room looks like
without me. I half hope he likes what he sees,

all that space.

DAY 296: QUIT

The weight is as heavy as a full bath,
and I know I am running out of metaphors to express
a scratch with no itch or a bandage with no wound to dress.

I feel as if I'm always being cruel to one thing or another,
but what? I want to be the kind of person that lets weight,
be weighty. There are versions of us that can become better

and because of that the opposite is also true.
What of that weight? Must I write about heaviness?
I am bored of myself and whatever line I'm about to write –

we know how it will feel when it ends and I quit.
The responsibility is yours to continue,
write a line to end this now, and take the weight.

DAY 297: CLEANSE

Everything falls out of my body
and she says, you should thank them
for bringing you here to this point,
and I think no, I shall thank the clouds
for showing me about life and not crushing me
with their weight on their way through.

DAY 298: CUT

The voice comes suddenly while I'm in the shower,
wrestling to wash my hair, but it's futile,
my hair will not clean, it has seen too much.

Years of weight and story swing from my small head,
it's so vast, that when I look in the mirror
it's all I can see.

Who is that person under there? Is it the person
reaching for the scissors to shed old layers,
feeling dead *and* alive?

Someone else's hands take mine and a rush of air
hits my neck. I inhale involuntarily as if my head
has just been baptised in water and at first,

there is the joy of rebellion as the hair
hits the floor wherever it wants, then
the tears fall and the grief swells,

changes are coming. I'm scared,
proud, and Cut. A voice says: *Leap
and the net will appear.*

I think it comes from my hand,
but it's my severed hair, the last chance
it has to save me from myself.

DAY 299: SOLD

Someone else can sell things
that don't belong to you
and you feel as if they did,
this house, my little house
in Calle Sanchez, goodbye
old friend, my first
and final refuge.

DAY 300: LETTER

It will make us better,
them knowing how we feel,

writing the letter,
makes us feel better,

sending them a letter
will make them feel better,

them knowing how we feel,
does not make us better,

we don't send the letter.

DAY 301: FORGIVEN

Vacancy: Explainer

Salary: A lifetime of peace

Essential: The ability to explain forgiveness

Desirable: Experience being the forgiver and forgiven

Responsibilities: To Kill

Please apply with your poem attached

References must come from those you've hurt or been hurt by

DAY 302: EPIPHANY

A prayer is the ask,
and you, the answer.

THEME: THRESHOLD

In the universe, there are things that are known,
and things that are unknown, and in between, there are doors.

William Blake

DAY 303: COCOON

Is there an alarm clock
inside a cocoon?

DAY 304: WHISPER

A whisper is not a spontaneous thing,
a whisper builds on the edge of the wind.

DAY 305: MIST

All I know is *me too* –
what is denser than water in the air?
I can't see beyond the reach of my arm,
are you there?

DAY 306: PAUSE

Take a moment to breathe with me,
what a year – I'm so proud of you,
our hearts are full, and so are our pages.

DAY 307: INTENTION

She says: *Ask yourself, what are your true intentions?*
Her gaze slides into my soul and lodges there,
she's still waiting for me to show.

DAY 308: POUR

A downpour of rain
resuscitates the dry earth,

boiling water poured into a mug
soothes a broken heart,

honey poured over pancakes
tells the morning we're in love.

DAY 309: PLANT

Everything is falling apart (or is it?),
apart, away, it's all the same,
I quit my job and planted strawberry seeds
which I'm determined not to kill.
Patience is the flower of perseverance –
like a muscle, it is exercised and cannot be born.
They say quitting my job to save my writing life
is impulsive, but I think it requires the utmost patience
to pursue. Planting seeds that may never grow,
which will never grow, if they aren't planted.

DAY 310: PONDER

The fold of a page asks for my attention,
in seat 162 on the *media distancia* train.

Squares of yellowish paper wink at me
from behind Gen Z jewellery.

She sits upright with a slight smile
as if my thoughts have moved her,

they haven't, she's found herself
in the pages of a book.

I ponder what sentence could be speaking to her,
from the canyon of history.

My fingers twitch. She glances over at me
as if the book had just told her she's being watched,

I fold the corner of an invisible page in the air.

DAY 311: JOURNAL

Ode to the Diary

Home of the secret crush and hedonistic tendencies,
home to hating those you don't really hate.
Home to the first love letter you never sent to your best friend,
the first hate mail you sent (and never meant) to your parents
because they read it, even though the words *KEEP OUT*
were scribbled in glitter gel pen, which is still to this day,
the strongest password ever.

Weapon against the deadly threat of being a teenager,
a hideaway to howl, build walls and hope, a cubicle to be emo,
cringe and ask embarrassing questions, another womb
to be innocent and brave, with no time for punctuation,
except exclamation marks.

DAY 312: MEDITATION

Sadguru said we have cannabis receptors,
which doesn't mean we were meant to ingest
but that being high is an inside job. Most didn't get it.
I roll out my mat, and my mind falls through my head
and out of my body, a tingling sensation creeps
across my chest, someone is inflating a balloon,
I feel myself smile, I am floating, nothing else,
flowers are blooming within in my arms and legs,
I want to laugh, my stomach grumbles,
I observe myself like a child getting a psych
evaluation, I get it.

DAY 313: GLIMMER

You finally knew what you had to do and began.
After 'The Journey' by Mary Oliver

The sun shines on the Sierra Mountains,
the soft lolloping slopes juxtapose jagged rock.
There is green as far as the eye can see
and you do not notice everything you're leaving.

You notice the single white cloud being worn like a hat
on the peak of a mountain. Two chairs and a picnic table
placed under a single tree, majestic chalk cliffs
that make you want to kneel and pledge your allegiance.

You admit the day didn't go as planned, but the breakfast,
the smile in your chest, that person who smiled back,
the same smile you glimpsed among the fields and olive groves
in the reflection of the glass the moment you knew.

DAY 314: FLOAT

This body, my buoy, my float – carry me.
I know this time will pass but I've the feeling
of drowning. My body in the sea is a fallen cloud,
that makes no splash or spray.

DAY 315: CHANNEL

In small and insignificant ways we connect with the future,
whilst remaining a conduit of the past.

Between the school runs, commutes and workouts,
we really are trying to try and listen.

Channelled message is what some use to describe a hook
or effective caption on social media

when they have something to say about the Universe
as if it began from their mouths.

.

I once heard someone say, *let life pass through you
as if you were a bamboo stick, hollow.*

But aren't we the flow? Most times, I'm certain
what I agree with, perhaps this is a channelled message.

DAY 316: CROSSROADS

Red fluffy caterpillars lay curled in the pavement cracks.
As I step over their frozen bodies, I pretend they're asleep.

What brought them here, of all places?
Out in the open, in the middle of the rush.

Perhaps they tried to escape the wilderness
until they saw why their ancestors kept them devolved.

Perhaps they're caterpillars whose lives were short
and they aren't trying to tell me something.

Why must I always see signs in nature?
Why must I always act upon seeing signs in nature?

I haul my shopping home, trying not to make this about me,
and I almost crash into a car.

I curl up on the pavement with all the questions
whirling around inside me.

I whisper to the Caterpillars, *which way to the wilderness?*
Quietly, so my boyfriend doesn't hear.

I think about the fact that spiders can dream,
that's old news, but do they interpret them?

Do they cast a web of meaning or follow
a silk thread that alters the course of their lives

because a fly happens to get caught in it?

Before I know it I'm back at the house,
I turn off the light and fall asleep.

The next morning I change my life.

DAY 317: BATHE

Who has the heart to tell my toes,
that they aren't gripping real grass?

I push my feet flat and firm against,
the white porcelain bath.

I push them to wake them up,
imagine them on the earth,
soaking up nutrients.

DAY 318: SING

You say *I can't sing*, and I ask,
where has your voice been left,
and at what age?

If you can't sing, how do you know
what being able to sing feels like?

You mean you don't sound
like the music artists on Spotify.

Do you sing in the shower?
Is that where it shines?

What is it you want to say,
or shout or cry?

Our body is the instrument,
our breath is the song,

there are truths inside of you,
waiting to be sung.

DAY 319: STIR

Before you realise a pot has been made,
we've sourced the ingredients, poured in our soul,
watched it steam, tended to the boil, tasted–tested,
and ladled into a bowl, we've seasoned it well,
and delivered with a smile.

DAY 320: RITUAL

To the God of Coffee,
I practice your scriptures daily,
bow to you at the dawn chorus,
and rise anew with your holy nectar
and biblical scent.

DAY 321: HONOUR

Honour the parts of you,
you had to leave
to get here.

DAY 322: GATHER

Women, I love you.
You got me through the darkest times,
and I don't know all the answers
to give light to yours, but I do know
the inevitable magic and healing
that arises when we gather.
Maybe this isn't a poem,
but maybe this is poetry.

DAY 323: MANTRA

It's so bad, it's impossible,
I hate it when that happens,
The problem is, words have magic.
The problem is a problem so bad,
it's impossible not to hate it when it happens.
Nam-myoho-renge-kyo
Every morning and night, changes your life.
It's possible to love it when it happens,
the solution is so incredible, words have magic,
the solution, I love it when that happens,
it's possible, it's incredible.

DAY 324: MAGIC

Confusion is a spell mid-cast, airborne,
that we stare intently at like a plant we've no idea
how to keep alive or a bomb about to explode.

We ask tentatively,
what have you been born to hunger for?
Where am I to put you, you half-formed thing?

But the spell is hurtling towards us,
and everything will soon fall into place.

DAY 325: DANCE

If in doubt, dance.

DAY 326: SPACE

Enter and know you've passed through a place
that doesn't care what ornaments adorn you,
nor for the declaration or confession of sins.

Come as you are, my arms will shield the rain,
my back, the storms, laughter is welcome here,
and returned to you in resounding echoes.

Some call me sanctuary, some call me refuge,
in truth I am a simple room, a space to go,
a place that loves you, with a door ajar.

DAY 327: INVITE

Just when I thought *this close* was close enough,
you entered the place where my soul hid,

invited me in, and showed me around
as if it were the most beautiful home

a person could live in,
is this mine?

DAY 328: GATE

Whatever you pray on, to, or with,
is a mirror pretending to be a gate.

Seek a mirror that reflects your seeking,
and there is no discovery but your current state –
seeking and so never enlightening,
and we do not rely on sight or knowledge
in the formless realm.

Do you want to seek,
or do you want to embody?
Polish your vision of tomorrow
not by what is in front of you,
but by what is *beyond*.

DAY 329: BOARDING

Where does the soul go during a seizure?

I'm pulling the bed away from the wall,
grabbing his phone, freezing at the sight
of the passcode – *how do I not know it by now?*

I see SOS in red letters, the kind of thing
you never think about until you need it.
There's blood, *I'm losing him.*

I open the door to an empty street.
Help will find us, I whisper as I return,
leaving the doors wide open in hope.

I stroke his back and turn him on his side,
checking his airways, relieved when I realise
the blood is just a bitten cheek.

I hold him as he moans a word
he'll never remember, and try with one hand
to keep the dog from licking the blood off his face,

and suddenly the spell breaks,
the room stops spinning

and the world is still and snoring.

It will be hours before he wakes, his Dad says.
I kiss his hand and I wait, and wait.
Where does a soul go during a seizure?

Into the body of those who have to watch,
 until eyelids flicker and their soul can return home
 – pulling a small piece of another's soul with it.

DAY 330: CUSP

Mountains are moving within me,
all you can see is skin and bone.

THEME: BEGINNINGS

Every new beginning comes from some other beginning's end.

Seneca the Younger

DAY 331: DAWN

On the train hurtling towards Cordoba,
the sun is a smudged rose ablaze in the sky.
I want to live somewhere the sunrises and sets.

I realise how little of these days I have left,
and how much time I spend staring at a lightbulb
above my head as if it will one day speak to me.

I want to live where the sunrises and sets,
everything else can wait.

DAY 332: DECIDE

Why are some things so easy to decide
and others like pulling teeth?
Perhaps the pain and the stalling
are part of the decision and necessary,
like a bicycle with stabilisers.

DAY 333: LEAP

A voice calls to me.
Leap and the net will appear.
When we help others, we create
an echo chamber and the help
reverberates off the walls
like a boomerang and hits us
straight in the face. The voice
sounds familiar.

DAY 334: AMATEUR

The best few weeks of your life,
big baller knowing nothing
of what you don't know.

DAY 335: PHONE CALL

On learning my dad had died

Hearing the words l*ion*,
eating the pavement *ant*,
walking to the hotel *elephant*,
ex trying to mount me, *stray cat.*

DAY 336: MEET-CUTE

The waitress smiles as she places
a *Cordadita* on the side, and says,

from my heart, in Spanish.

Her eyes are steady and shining,
her hands a blur of movement.

I stir the coffee creme and make
the shape of a cartoon heart.

Before the heart is finished,
the creme curves into a woman's face,

and then a sailing boat, a snake,
and a tiny baby in the womb.

I stop stirring. I take a sip,
it tastes a little bitter, a little wrong.

DAY 337: NEWS

When they told me there was nothing to do,
nothing to be done, I did nothing,
and nothing carried on.

DAY 338: LAUNCH

They are launching poetry into space,
which I got excited about until I realised
the first dog went into orbit in 1957.

When I phoned NASA, they explained,
that it takes longer to domesticate poems.
But I told them - there's no need to spend

millions of dollars teaching a poem *flight*,
they're born for lift-off. So get your pens ready,
they want fifty by morning light.

DAY 339: PROMOTION

I promoted myself to Executive Director
and registered *My Life* on Companies House.

I hired a room, invited old managers,
but no one came except my dog,

so we went for a walk
because we could, we had time.

We had one of those meetings
execs are meant to have,

butt clenched walking laps
around the park in lycra.

We stopped for coffee and cake
because we could, we had time

and saw a young man drawing
with a paper sign that said:

Hire me, I'd like to pay for college.

So I called myself and asked,

do I have time to meet with this lad?

And my dog said yes, sat down
and took the minutes.

His designs were amazing,
and we talked about his life,

I bought into him,
more than his marketing style,

he called his mum and told her
he'd make her something nice.

We smiled as we said goodbye
and called it a day because we could,

we had time.

DAY 340: RESULTS

It's for the best

It wasn't the ideal timing.
I cried when I learned I carried

a bloated nothing, a concoction
of chemicals causing chaos in my cervix.

Losing nothing felt worse,
than losing something.

Why do I feel like I was a Mother
before I was born?

Trying to find my way back
to my children in every life.

DAY 341: ADDITION

In addition:

Poetry is the seed, and the writing life is the soil, but there is a third, a divine presence. It is the observer witnessing the germination process, showing up to water and nurture where needed, but not getting in the way. You could also call this the Universe, but it is one and the same, you are the Universe working through you. This is the Poet, where they veer towards the great sages of the earth and at the same moment become a humble gardener, a caretaker of something begot of them but that does not belong to them. It is to carry the knowledge that whatever comes from, is at once beyond. This is why Poets are the greatest teachers of our lifetime, the great channellers to our divine connection with life, and they must be protected and supported at all costs.

DAY 342: GRADUATE

Lincoln Cathedral 2011,
blue dress and black hat,
my dad in a wheelchair.

Dad, I got a First!

A smile folding into a face.

*Great, when am I going to
watch you in Doctor Who?*

The Future pushing
the wheelchair down
Steep Hill forever.

DAY 343: BACKPACKING

I wonder how far women would have gone
if they weren't so good at holding things.

DAY 344: INTRODUCTION

I come from Gobblefunk and Zozimus,
grease and roast dinners,
pogo sticks, and pub gardens

I come from poo sticks thrown off bridges.

I come from family trips to Southend on Sea,
comb-overs and Tamagotchi,
Ocean eyes and Pokemon cards,

I come from endless cups of tea.

I come from champion indoor tent makers,
Spice Girls, and tape recorders,
theme parks made out of mattresses,

I come from egg and spoon races.

I come from remembrance parades,
summer fetes and smashing plates,
wishing my Dad was more like Amy's Dad,

I come from bike rides over the way.

I come from Poppadoms and Pick a Mix,
the magic pen of C.S Lewis, I come from 196
and the threads of mum's blanket.

DAY 345: BOOK

Children are still climbing into their parents' wardrobes
pulling on huge fur coats, knocking on the back wall,
hoping for a glimpse of snow.

Children are still eyeballing a glass of water,
as white knuckles clutch the countertop,
come on glass, tip over.

There will still be children dressed in trench coats,
calling themselves Inspector Gadget,
because an adult believed

a book could translate magic.

DAY 346: CELEBRATE

If today was your three hundred and forty-fourth birthday,
how would you celebrate?

DAY 347: INVEST

Sometimes it's hard to invest
Nothing to make something.

How do you get that little bit
of breathing space, without
a freak accident of nature
or someone else's death?

DAY 348: INHERIT

Your DNA is the culmination
of hundreds of thousands of people
who loved each other.

Long after he died, I noticed him living.
Which meant more than when my mum told me
I'd just missed out on my inheritance, £80,000.

I felt no grief, there was no loss
in losing the nothing I already had,
but when I saw his hands reach for my pen,

grief and joy danced up my arms,
hairs standing on end.

DAY 349: ADOPT

We always have these conversations in bed,
after sex, or tired from the day's end.

If we wrote your name in Alphabetti Spaghetti,
scattered it in petals, or danced the letters into the sand,
it would feel like a birth and not a grave rescue.

You don't know we exist, but we're coming for you,
like water to a burning house.

DAY 350: SKILL

When an archer shoots for a target,
they aim at themselves.

This male is the arrow
and the female is the bow.

Together they live a life
committed to the shoot,

to find out how skilled they are
at being an arrow and a bow,

how committed they are
to being themselves,

and seeing themselves
in the other.

It's all just a game
until the arrow hits,

because if it hits twice,
it's a skill.

DAY 351: UNION

We lay there in the dark,
and when the silence settles
he says, does it feel...
like you're losing yourself?
I barely get the word out.

Elation and devastation reign,
I know that I'm not alone.

DAY 352: SPRING

Red curtains open to a day in Spring,
I'm reading this poetry book to my baby,
a man in a long white gown, a holy man of sorts,
sits cross-legged on a mat as if his joints
were made of oil. His bare feet shine
in the sun-dappled light.

As I read, multi-coloured poems bloom
out of my mouth like flower petals
and the baby laughs and tries to catch them.

DAY 353: BIRTH

Five days after my dad died,
my god-daughter was born.
As his final words fell into my dreams,
I knew we'd meet again,
and that he'd return soft,
as soft as peaches and as kind
as Librarians.

DAY 354: BLOOM

When a flower is late to bloom,
do we blame the flower?

Or do we look at its environment
and ask what it needs?

What do you need little flower?

DAY 355: FRUIT

When I feel broken or that life is unripe or rotten,
I remember a whole orange is segmented, soft enough
to put a confident thumb through, and still delicious.

THEME: GRATITUDE

*Gratitude makes sense of our past, brings peace for today,
and creates a vision for tomorrow.*

Melody Beattie

A Note on Gratitude

Amazing work, you've almost completed an entire year of prompts! Now is the time to thank yourself. You've come a long way since you first picked up this book. For the next three days, I want you to thank your past, present and future self for getting here. I've only done so much, you're the one who has shown up for yourself and your writing practice, so give yourself some love.

If it feels strange to write about yourself, write from a friend's perspective or try writing about a friend you admire. Then read the poem aloud as if it were written about you. I hope you know how far you've come and that you spend as much time as possible over the next few days honouring the writer that you had to become to get here.

DAY 356: PAST

Thank you, little lady,
who believed she could write
the entire world down.

You were onto something.

DAY 357: PRESENT

You are a book being written,
and you've opened to this page,
with no page before and after,
just what this page says.

It says *you are a writer,*
because you write today.

DAY 358: FUTURE

Thank you for becoming everything
you've become to make dreams come true.

You who shoulders the weight
of the questions and doubt,

you who knows more than I,
and still listens, *thank you.*

Thank you for never giving up,
and writing a path to freedom.

THEME: REFLECTION

Without reflection, we go blindly on our way.

Margaret J. Wheatley

A Note on Reflection

How did that feel, to thank yourself? In seven days we will have been writing together for a year. You may be a different person now compared with the person who started this book, I've certainly changed. It's important at this moment, to take stock of just how far you've come and reflect on what got you here.

The aim is to approach the coming year with a better idea of who you are as a writer, how you want to write, and where you want your writing to take you. This is a mulching of the soil, you've planted so many beautiful seeds, so let's gather our wisdom and tools, and prepare for the harvest.

I've curated the following prompts to help you articulate the challenges you've grown through, discover what was easy or difficult, and ponder why particular poems or prompts resonated. I've included a series of questions for you to answer as well as my own reflections on the past year. Read my responses before answering the questions yourself to spark some insight, or answer the questions first and then see what I've written – you may be surprised at how similar our answers are.

If you're new to journaling, I'd recommend spending a few minutes on each question and writing whatever comes into your head. Use the ten minutes to write your questions or write on the prompt as normal and then reflect afterward. Share your answers using #plantyourpoetry online or pop me an email, I'd love to know what you unearthed.

DAY 359: REVEL

The horse bends its head
to drink from the clear water,
thankful for a tongue.

What were your favourite single poetry prompts to write on, and why?

I loved writing on the JAM, LIFELINE, BRUNCH and GROW prompts. These poems brought me great joy because they were personable but could offer something of use to the reader too. These are my favourite kind of poems to write.

What were your favourite themed prompts to write on, and why?

I loved writing on the theme of LANGUAGE. It was so much fun to play with form and language within a poem. It's easy to forget that poems or writing in general can be fun. We're often made to feel like we have to be hard at it, pouring our grief onto the page. but language has a lightness and humour too, just like life. I also enjoyed writing on the theme of THRESHOLD. It resonated with my life perfectly at the time of writing. I'm a spiritual and curious soul interested in the magic in the every day. Poets are often naturally inclined to write about this subject because they are poetic in and of themselves. I felt like I was writing some magic into the world.

Which poem got the best response if shared?

People loved JAM because they could relate it to their own family times around the table. Nearly every household has a memory associated with a jar of goodness and it can evoke a myriad of memories and poems.

What is your favourite poem and why?

One of my favourite poems is GROW, there is something about Wildflowers that makes me feel spirited. I used to be concerned about what others thought of me and would take it personally when being myself triggered others. Now I'm too busy focusing on joy and growing to worry about all that.

What was the kindest or most touching comment about your poetry this year?

Someone had lost his wife and was trying to get back into writing to help with the grieving process. He messaged to tell me that I was a major part of his return to and starting his blog, which touched me deeply.

What strengths would you say you developed or noticed about yourself?

I'm very good at thinking on my feet. I think I'm much better at sponta-neous marketing and idea creation. I didn't plan all of this years before, I've only had the idea to do this book around six months ago, some prompts I came up with on the day and it all just seemed to work out. I noticed that I'm a bit obsessed, which I love. It's my thing, I do it well and it aligns with my values. That is a strength in my opinion. I also realised how much I cared, this care carried me on when my mind or body couldn't.

How did you benefit from writing on the prompts and what did you learn?

Most of my thoughts on this are included in the front of the book, but writing on the prompts accelerated an understanding of what my purpose is. Everything that didn't serve my writing had to go. I became much better at setting boundaries with others and with myself. I learned that I'm not a quitter and that with helpful systems and beliefs in place, anything is possible.

Why should you continue writing this year, on prompts or otherwise?

Because I feel this is just the beginning and that I can reach and help more people. I am becoming a better person through this and I'm excited and terrified of the future like I'm teetering on the cusp of something audacious.

What advice would you give your future self based on what went well or worked out for you?

Keep going, this is working. Don't be too hard on yourself, and don't forget to enjoy life whilst writing about it.

DAY 360: CONFRONT

Fly at the window
trying to buzz its way through
a closed window pane.

What were your least favourite single poetry prompts to write on, and why?

I'd say the broader prompts were more challenging such as FEAR, WOUND, and DARKNESS because there are so many things to write about. I gave up trying to pin down such epic concepts into one poem and began with one simple detail.

What were your least favourite themed prompts to write on, and why?

I struggled with the FAMILY theme. Trying to encapsulate a human being in a poem is daunting. What if someone has a different truth? I began small and chose simple moments or characteristics to build the poems around, rather than making the whole person into a poem.

What did you find most difficult on this journey and why was that?

I found it difficult to think about anything else. It highlighted everything that wasn't aligned with my writing, living in a city and working in a school were no longer tolerable. The trouble was the job had given me a contract

424

and a visa to be in a country that was now my home. I was torn between quitting my job and being forced to return to the UK with nowhere to go, or staying where I was and letting go of my book dream. Turns out these weren't the only options, the universe provided me with a middle way.

I also realised it wasn't about how bad the job or the city was, but how essential writing was. This helped to shift my focus from what I didn't want, to what I did want and the contrast initiated the changes required to finish this book, so I'm glad it happened.

Did you notice a period of 'not-writing', what caused it?

DAY: 83 to DAY: 102 were difficult for me because a lot was changing. It was May 2023 and my first placement ended in Spain, a placement in a school that I loved and I had to move out of my beloved apartment. I said goodbye to a dear friend and reluctantly returned to London for the summer.

What got you writing again?

Reaching out for help and asking my best friend Daisy to write with me. She supported me in releasing the poetry prompts for a while and introducing the weekly themed prompts was her idea. Her injection of love and energy kick-started me back into gear in an uncertain time, I believed in my abilities again. How to keep writing during turbulent times would make a good chapter in a book, if not an entire book in itself.

What was your biggest fear/s when starting this journey and what helped you navigate through and continue writing?

The fear was cumulative. There was nothing to be fearful of at first because there were no stakes but that's what time, effort, and visibility can do, it can make us start to care about how we've spent that time, and if we're doing it better, which gets us in our heads.

My inner critic kept telling me that I wasn't doing it for the 'right' reasons and that I was doing it because I felt I needed validation and reassurance/visibility. I was afraid I wasn't good enough or known enough to take responsibility for something like this. I was afraid I'd give up and let everyone down.

What helped me was to understand that fears are valid, but they aren't reasons not to write. Writing about those fears helped to shed light on shame and re-focusing my attention on what I was excited about helped to shift that energy. I met my demons, acknowledged their presence, and let them squabble whilst I was moving forward word by word, they soon got bored.

Another thing that got me through was every single person who shared a poem and wrote to me to thank me and tell me how it was helping them.

What got in the way of building your writing habit or writing poems this year?

Self-doubt and criticism. A lack of boundaries on days when I was tired or in an environment that did not inspire me creatively. Sometimes I hid behind helping others to avoid writing. Writing 365 poems in one year and publishing a book about it was either an amazing idea or madness - probably a bit of both.

What advice would you give yourself when facing the above fears or challenges?

Remember why you do this, and how it feels to not be doing it. Remember every single person whose life you have shifted in some small or big way. Remember how it feels to look back not having given up and how thankful you were. Remember this every time you feel like it would be easier to stop.

DAY 361: OFFER

Acorn leaps from tree
into your half-open hands
hoping it's enough.

What poem or piece of writing resonated with you this year that was written by someone else, and why?

I was consistently blown away by the alacrity in which Peter Niu wrote such incisive poems in a flash. I know nothing about them except everything they shared in their writing. There was this sense of the burn and the beauty in their noticing of life and humanity, that was delivered with such specificity and tenderness. Go and follow them on Instagram @missingthepoint and if someone doesn't publish them soon, I will.

Who or what gave you the strength to carry on when things got tough?

The Winter Writing Sanctuary 22-23 who wrote on the prompts every day. The incredible community of writers on Instagram, my partner, mum, writing bestie and dog. Fresh air, plenty of coffee and tea. Dragging myself away from the laptop to remember the smell of blossom and grass. The prompts themselves, the regularity of them. The feeling that it's now or never, the loss of people close to me, reminding me of the impermanence of life.

What would you tell this person if you could?

I'd tell them that when I felt I wasn't good enough to do this, their belief in me changed the tide.

What qualities did you find in others you'd like to embody in yourself next year?

I'd like to embody a quiet resolve and the ability to disappear for a while and know that the writing life won't disappear. I'd like to wander more and engage more deeply with the poetic voice, I tend to trip over my feet rushing to finish things or come up with new ideas.

What did you learn from other writers this year?

Asking for help is necessary and sometimes people need to be asked. You can help someone just as much by asking them for their insight, or skills - people love to be asked, and those same people may struggle with asking or approaching you.

What makes a generous and supportive writer?

Someone who organically adds to the ecosystem. Someone who isn't always thinking of what they can get but what they can give. Someone who has forgiven themselves and has compassion for the path, and what it asks of us.

DAY 362: ASK

Tiny Mouse asks Cat
how to meow as a Mouse,
cat considers it.

What about the writing world do you feel you have no idea about?

I have little knowledge of what it's like to be inside a publishing house
or part of a small press. I have a dream of being a book editor, mainly in
non-fiction and poetry or curating anthologies and works that other people
have written. I have very little knowledge about how this is done, I need to
get asking!

Working with a literary agent, a part of me is extremely curious, but a part
of me wants to see how far I can get off my own volition (and harbours a
tiny belief that I don't deserve one yet).

Write three things you would like help with on your writing journey.

1. I designed and formatted this book cover and the interior manuscript
   using a free book formatting service, although I'm pleased with how it
   turned out, I'd love a little more freedom. I could either upskill, learn
   Adobe Photoshop or the basics of graphic design or give back to the
   community by paying freelancers for their skills. In the future, I'd love
   to have some of these things covered so I could focus on the writing

more, this probably means help putting together a budget or raising money to pay those freelancers well for their time. I'm hoping this book will help me to invest in that.

2. I'd love someone to take me step by step (working backward from the book release date) through the project management side of a book, with a focus on marketing. To show me how to optimise my time and build a strategy to carry my inspiration and ideas to fruition.

3. Submitting to foundations and bursaries to support my writing time. I am very good at finding opportunities for other people, which I love and never want to stop doing. I'd just like to get a little push to do the same for myself.

Name three people you can reach out to and ask for help and support.[*]

1. A very special mentor and accomplished book author.
2. A person with experience in editing poetry and curating works.
3. Someone with a lot of experience in applying for funding.

[*]Names have been omitted for privacy.

Where else can you find the answers to improve your writing life?

Read more! Put out polls on social media and send emails, ask questions and get answers from those with lived experience. Keep up with my discovery journal and read back over my notes and posts that I share to support other writers.

What scares you most about asking for help?

I'm scared of being preyed on, repeating old patterns where I reach out to others only to end up feeding someone else's ego and lining their pockets. I'm nervous about getting mixed up in something I can't get out of easily, this must have to do with trust. I'm scared to be used, scared to be helped only if I can pay a fee, which almost always can't happen because I'm living hand to mouth.

Perhaps I'm scared that if I ask and receive help, I won't be able to tell myself I can do it on my own anymore, perhaps I'm afraid of being vulnerable, of being seen, of someone having power over my life and freedom.

Looking at it like this, I'm not surprised I feel all this considering what I've been through. But I'm doing so well (and so are you), let's remind ourselves of that.

My intuition is strong and the trust in myself and the Universe has helped me so much this year. She has been showing up with exactly what I need and I thank her often.

How would you benefit if you received that help? How would it help your writing life?

I could reach more people, write better quality work, manage my time and make decisions based on flow and not fear. I could find a collaboration that elevates both my life, their life and the lives of those around us. If I received that help it wouldn't just be my writing life that would change, I'd make sure to pay it forward.

DAY 363: SELECT

Bee hovers above
the scantily clad roses,
chooses today's feast.

Select three poems you like from this past year that may have something worth submitting or pursuing further. Why did you choose these three?

1. DAY 260: EARTHQUAKE - I like the imagery and the universality that we're all going about our lives in seemingly insignificant ways whilst experiencing births and deaths of seismic proportions, daily, without talking to each other about them.
2. DAY 172: COLOSSUS - Sometimes we are gods and sometimes mortal. We can feel as if we are forever being pushed and pulled in either direction.
3. DAY 175: DIONYSUS, GOD OF FESTIVITY - I love that this poem spills out of itself and as a result, carries the reader like wine being poured out until it's empty. I'm interested in observing the part of humanity that secretly wants everything to fall apart so we can feel more righteous, and placate our self-tormented souls with things that feel good. I'm amused yet unsettled by it, this makes for a great muse.
4. DAY 316: CROSSROADS AND 245: SISTER could be strong contenders too, they make me feel like I'm heading in the right direction.

What poem would you gift a friend going through a hard time?

DAY 354: BLOOM or DAY 326: SPACE

What poem would you send a family member to show them how much they're loved?

DAY 229: MINT – I've noticed that I've written a few poems about my cousin who sadly passed away, all of them trying to bridge the gap between life and loss, all poems I wish he could listen to, poems to pull him back from the brink.

Which poem would you send a colleague to make them laugh?

DAY 264: ACCENT

Which poem would you gift an aspiring writer or poet to encourage them?

DAY 341: ADDITION, DAY 218: THE MAGICIAN and DAY 220: THE HERMIT

What common themes arose in your work?

Grief, love, nature, transformation. I'm keen to hear the readers' thoughts on what themes jumped out to them.

What three words sum up your experience writing one poem per day, or what poems encapsulated the journey you went on?

In this order.

1. DAY 331: LEAP
2. DAY 305: MIST
3. DAY 161: DAMSEL / DAY 220: THE HERMIT

DAY 364: INVENT

A lost baby bird
uses a twig to prop him,
and learns to fly anew.

What prompt or themed prompts weren't included that you would like to have written on?

Story genres would have been fun, and food. I'll make sure to add them in the next book!

In what three places can you find prompt words (excluding prompt books or other people's prompts)?

1. Immediate surroundings, look and name everything you see. For example: Window, plant, table, paper, blinds, curtain.
2. Any book to hand, open the book at a random page and choose the first word that jumps out at you. Using a dictionary is a great way to grow your vocabulary and learn the definitions of interesting words.
3. A random word generator online.

Use one of those methods now, what prompt did you come up with?

Mug.

How did it feel to come up with your own prompt/s? Was it easy or difficult?

It came to me very quickly, I used the 'take in your surroundings' method and didn't even have to get up off my chair. I began to think of everything a mug holds, which brought various memories to the surface. Laughs with loved ones, arguments and heartbreaks, revelations. I feel a poem brewing.

For the book, it was a lot easier than you'd think. Many of the prompt words led to other words just by association. Coming up with themes and then prompts on those themes was a little more challenging but also kept it interesting. There are around one million words in the English language, that's a million prompts, a million seeds of poems waiting to be planted.

DAY 365: VISION

A rose deflowers,
shedding for tomorrow's bloom,
becoming herself.

This time next year, how would you want your writing practice to look, what would you be writing, where and/or who with?

I would like a little more structure in place to manage the periods of quiet, financially speaking. I would like to live a more sustainable and autonomous lifestyle to continue writing out in nature more regularly. I would love to start a writing group that regularly writes outside together. I want to explore my non-fiction book project. I'd like to offer a few bonus extras alongside this book. I'd like to learn more about using audible and audio in my future work. I'd love to go to Japan, near Kyoto, to a silent retreat centre I've had my eye on, with nothing but a notebook and pen. I'd like to submit a poetry collection and a non-fiction proposal to a traditional publisher.

Okay, I'm taking a breath because I could go on forever with *things*.

1. I'd like my writing practice to look: joyful, healing, and liberating.
2. I'd be writing from the heart, deeply, authentically and with wonder.
3. I'd be writing in a slow-paced environment, somewhere that makes me feel safe and at peace, connected and surrounded by nature.

What would help you to get to this point? List three long-term goals and three daily habits to help you grow your writing habit.

Long-term.

1. Find a place that engenders a more sustainable way of living and relocate
2. Live a life completely in the service of poetry and those who it touches
3. Work with a traditional publisher and agent on my next project

Short-term.

1. Research! Spend 20 minutes researching one element of my vision
2. Show up at my desk for at least twenty minutes every day
3. Read one poem from another writer every day

If someone gave you a year to write with enough money to live off, how and where would you spend it?

I'd show up at my desk, write my way toward a flourishing life, and help others to do the same.

I'd love the opportunity and support to deeply research a topic, to arrange interviews, meet inspiring people, and travel to places to aid my writing.

I'd rent a villa somewhere in Spain in Andalucia and give as many writers free board and food and share the gift of unencumbered time as far as I could.

How can you nourish your mind, body and spirit this next year to support your writing habit?

Start my own vegetable garden. Eat well and drink lots of water. Keep stretching and practising yoga. Make sure I take regular breaks from writing to go outside or dance. Make sure I re-enter the world where I can and give it some love. Remember to maintain presence when I'm not at my desk working and not just think about writing.

What skills can you acquire or who can you reach out to support you with your vision for the next year?

1. Workaways, retreats or holdings that will welcome a poet willing to do some graft
2. Gardening skills!
3. Like-minded people whose vision is aligned

What emotions, fears, or doubts came up when answering these questions?

It's kind of scary, to admit what you want. To write stuff down and not come close to the end of the list of things you want to embrace in this one wild and precious life. What if the things you've written down turn out to be the wrong thing? What about the things you didn't write down, will they never happen?

I know my experiences aren't unique and that you're here because you feel the pull too. I share with the knowledge that maybe not everything will happen, or should happen in the way I imagine, but that by having a vision and moving toward it day by day, I can tread a path and shine a light for you to follow when you find yourself lost.

Afterword

Does anyone else feel like they've walked a marathon? I suddenly notice how tired I am. It dawned on me the day after finishing this book, that a little tender loving care was needed after such a long walk. So I wanted to offer some support and assurances that helped me, in case you're feeling a little bereft.

I felt a wave of grief when the prompts ended, but I found comfort in the knowledge that it was necessary to make space for something just as magical to arrive. I'm proud, excited, and nervous as to the impact this book will have and what doors it will open. Seneca the Younger put it best when he said that, *every new beginning comes from some other beginning's end.*

Feeling like you need a holiday or a break, mixed with feeling like you never want this to finish is normal. It's like having to say goodbye to a character in a fiction book who dies at the end or turning the last page of a well-loved book that doesn't yet have a sequel. I'm sure I will have come up with another slightly mad idea that will feature writing on prompts for the next year by the time you've reached this point, so keep faith.

If you have been writing alongside me in the Facebook group, I will answer any questions and offer support, perhaps we can collate all the pieces we have written and do something beautiful with them. Maybe you'd like to turn your year of poems into a poetry collection, or perhaps you need

439

time to process. If a period of silence arrives, it's natural to feel a little unsettled. Reach out to someone you trust in the writing world, someone who understands - this is an important part of the creative process.

I hope this journey has brought you closer to the voice that calls to you from beyond the edges of your life, the voice that is desperate for you to catch up with it, the one that never stops whispering, *you are a writer*.

* * *

Keep in touch via email at a_poetontheroad@outlook.com or social media, it would mean the world to hear your experiences and read your poems. I have a bouquet of ideas for nurturing the garden we're tending to - this isn't the end, I promise.

Acknowledgments

I've planted 365 original poems and prompts into this book, but the process was more like being part of a community allotment. It took a village, which you were a central part of. The poetry community is the reason this book came to fruition.

I owe the most credit to Beth Kempton, author of Kokoro, The Way of the Fearless Writer and founder of Do What You Love. Meeting her catapulted my writing life into orbit through her free Winter Writing Sanctuaries and her #tinyspringpoem challenge. She made it extremely difficult for me to continue as normal as if I wasn't meant for this. Thank you, Beth, for being a light.

Special thanks go to everyone in the Winter Writing Sanctuary 22-23 who wrote alongside me over the past year, offering their encouragement, poems and gratitude for my prompts - I thank you from the bottom of my heart.

My darling Daisy, my go-to writing and editing buddy, thank you for carrying me through some of the toughest times this year and refusing to visit me so I wouldn't have an excuse not to finish this book.

To my Mum and first choice editor. Returning my A* essay to my teacher because it had spelling errors wasn't wasted, thank you for your unwavering love and support. Any typos in this book must have been added after.

To Jess, for your gentle strength and sharp editing insight, you were the person I needed most in my formative years as a poet.

To Patrick, for showing up every day with love and endless cups of tea/food/jokes/hugs. I did mean it when I said I might have died of starvation in the final week if you hadn't fed me. I love you.

To all writers sharing their experiences on the writing life on the internet and in books for no other reason than to make the path a little easier to tread for those that follow, you saved me time and tears and I'm eternally grateful.

About the Author

Louise Goodfield, also known as A Poet on the Road, is an award-winning published poet, performer and creative facilitator from the UK.

Her poems have been published in numerous magazines and anthologies. She is Little Bird's Publishing House's Flash Friday Winner and has performed her poetry across the UK and Europe.

Since 2018, Louise has developed and delivered poetry workshops for schools, charities, festivals, retreats, and arts organisations in the UK and Europe. She is currently running an online Writing Poetry and Submitting Poetry Course. She was awarded a Developing Your Creative Practice Grant by Arts Council England to empower vulnerable communities through poetry. She is an Apples & Snakes emerging writers' alumni, where she received mentorship from Joelle Taylor, Adam Kammerling, and Francesca Beard.

Louise is co-founder of the collaborative poetry collective Tandem Poets, which seeks to elevate the lives and work of artists through co-authored poems and creative collaboration.

Join the private Plant Your Poetry Facebook group and write alongside Louise and other writers around the globe who are planting their poetry one day at a time. Click the link below or type the address into your browser and add your order receipt details.

You can connect with me on:

- https://www.facebook.com/groups/724207669903452
- https://www.facebook.com/plantyourpoetry
- https://www.instagram.com/a_poetontheroad
- https://linktr.ee/a_poetontheroad
- https://www.facebook.com/poetontheroad
- https://www.plantyourpoetry.com
- https://www.louisegoodfield.co.uk

Subscribe to my newsletter:

- https://substack.com/@apoetontheroad

Printed in Great Britain
by Amazon

41518924R00258